A Ligh
Wisd

How to Read the Inspired Books

Also by James A. Fischer
published by Paulist Press

INTERPRETING THE BIBLE
LOOKING FOR MORAL GUIDANCE (out of print)

A Lighthearted View of Wisdom in the Bible

How to Read the Inspired Books

James A. Fischer, C.M.

PAULIST PRESS
New York/Mahwah, N.J.

Artwork by Mary Ingenthron

Cover design by Lynn Else

Library of Congress Cataloging-in-Publication Data

Fischer, James A.
    A lighthearted view of wisdom in the Bible : how to read the inspired books / James A. Fischer.
        p. cm.
    Includes bibliographical references (p.) and index.
    ISBN 0-8091-4052-7 (alk. paper)
    1. Wisdom literature—Criticism, interpretation, etc. I. Title.

BS1455 .F57 2001
223′.06—dc21

                                                      2001052304

Published by Paulist Press
997 Macarthur Boulevard
Mahwah, New Jersey 07430

www.paulistpress.com

Printed and bound in the
United States of America

Contents

Abbreviations

AB	*Anchor Bible,* Garden City, N.Y.: Doubleday.
ANET	J. B. Pritchard, ed., *Ancient Near Eastern Texts Relating to the New Testament*. Princeton: Princeton University Press, 1950; 3rd ed. with supplement, 1978.
CBQ	*Catholic Biblical Quarterly*
JBL	*Journal of Biblical Literature*
LXX	Septuagint
NAB	New American Bible
NT	New Testament
NTSt	*New Testament Studies*
OT	Old Testament
RSR	*Religious Studies Review*
SBLDS	Society of Biblical Literature Dissertation Series. Atlanta: Scholars Press.
TDNT	G. Kittel and G. Friedrich, eds., *Theological Dictionary of the New Testament,* 10 Vols. (GR, 1964–76)
VT	*Vetus Testamentum*

To my teachers:
the people of God,
the participants of numerous Bible discussion groups
who have taught me wisdom

Prologue

"Proverbs are made by wise men and repeated by fools, but the proverb that explains a proverb has never been found." So begins the introduction to the *Oxford Book of English Proverbs*. We all know a proverb when we hear one, but we can't put our finger on a neat definition. Riddles, parables, conundrums, maxims, picturesque sayings, meditations—they will all fit. No author is ever given. Proverbs are the people's language. They come from the people's experience. They are usually shrewd and they are often witty.

> *A lazy man is no better than a dead one, but he takes up more room.*

Proverbs may also be platitudinous and dull but we learn not to repeat these lest we be found fools.

Every culture seems to have proverbs and collects them. They share much in common. They are all colored by each culture and even more by the worldview that stands behind them. They prove nothing; they can be disputed without fear, and yet they probably will persuade in the end. They have a necessary function. We say: "If anything can go wrong, it will." How does Murphy's law function? We really don't care who

1

Murphy was or whether he ever existed. But when we have a streak of bad experiences, we can console ourselves by saying that it is perfectly normal. It helps us survive and keep going.

This is rhetoric, and its function is to persuade us to act. Rhetoric has a bad name today as a deliberate attempt to manipulate us by distortion of the truth, but it has an ancient and noble heritage. It is the art of persuasion. It may defy logic and still move us to action; in its evil form it can deliberately misdirect us.

The Bible has a book called Proverbs. Proverbs occurs in the third of the divisions of the Jewish collections, namely, the Law, the Prophets and the Writings. Five books of the Writings are usually called wisdom books, namely, Job, Proverbs, Ecclesiastes, Sirach and Wisdom of Solomon. Many fragments of the same kind of writing are found in other places in the Bible—stories of creation, Jonah, sections of John's Gospel and Paul's letters, to mention a few. Proverbs are the basic building blocks of all this wisdom.

Scholars have concentrated on unraveling the sources of these sayings, their precise literary forms and some overall theme in whole books. This has been very useful for the scholars but has not always helped the average reader to understand what one is supposed to get out of them for daily living. The Book of Job has always fascinated readers about its treatment of unmerited evil but remains a mystery. Ecclesiastes is quizzical about accomplishments in life. Yet in reading these books, a light may suddenly shine on us as we recognize a familiar conviction from our own experience. It may also beckon us to project our visions farther than we expected.

I have attempted here to take a different approach to this people's wisdom. This is a rhetorical approach, which demands that the reader exercise imagination. So much antithesis abounds in proverbs that we can often see our own real-life experiences revealed. The people who first fashioned these proverbial sayings often endured a difficult world. Sometimes God appeared hostile or indifferent, but in the long run God was smiling and indulgent. We can then measure our own paradoxical experiences of the world from our own contemporary viewpoint against their larger wisdom. Then our thoughts can soar. Our projections can take us up to the heavens if we are willing to go. Perhaps we can even discover the face of God behind this common wisdom. The people of God canonized it as the Word of God.

Jacob at Bethel had a vision of a ladder going up to heaven and God's messengers going up and down. The Word of God can still reveal to us a way to climb the ladder that rests on the firm earth of experience but reaches into the heavens. This people's wisdom still functions today if we will listen.

Rev. James A. Fischer, C.M.

1

The Underpinnings of Wisdom

1. Rhetorical Communication

A number of very good books have appeared in recent years on wisdom literature—Leo Perdue, *Wisdom and Creation;* Roland Murphy, *The Tree of Life;* and William Brown, *Character in Crisis.*[1] These are "state of the art" developments mostly from historical criticism. They are most helpful. Perdue and the others survey older works and classify authors by their differing themes, such as creation, anthropology, character formation, cosmology and theodicy. A small outreach to rhetorical criticism also appears; for example, Leo Perdue elaborates on the function of metaphor, and William Brown uses narrative criticism to construct a plot and to diagnose characters. Roland Murphy wittily quotes G. K. Chesterton: "God says, in effect, that if there is one fine thing about the world, as far as men are concerned, it is that it cannot be explained. The whole is a sort of psalm or rhapsody on the sense of wonder. The maker of all things is astonished at the things He has Himself made."[2] But despite all these efforts we do not as yet have a bona fide rhetorical criticism method in hand. Can we begin to devise such an alternative method?

2. The Underpinnings of Rhetoric

First I would set forth some preliminaries on reader-response theory that form the psychological and literary underpinnings of rhetoric for persuading us to accept the fittingness in addition to the logical. A reader-response approach is a literary study of how a text channels the reader into making a response that the author anticipates. How the mind works in responding needs some background understanding.

3. The Psychological Underpinnings

Paul Watzlawick and his team in Palo Alto, California, used the term *metacommunication* to understand patients with psychological problems.[3] Metacommunication is the communication that lies "beside" or "under" what the words say. It is a good term for my purpose. Very simplistically, the medical data begins with the functions of the right and left hemispheres of the brain. The left hemisphere deals mostly in digital operations; the right in analogic activities. Although the words seem vaguely familiar from computer talk, they are much older. *Digital* comes from "digit" or "finger" and refers to small bits of information. *Analogic* refers to "analogy," the ability to express one idea in terms of another. In a rough way, the left brain is logical and the right brain is poetic. The right brain puts together an overview of the whole by closing the gaps. This is an oversimplification, of course, but it gives us a rule of thumb to begin working with.

Watzlawick and his associates discovered in their clinical practice that a prime difficulty in treating patients lay with communication. "Where are you coming from?" is the psychologist's first problem in diagnosing the illness of the client. The data and logic of the left brain of the patient does not seem to be processed normally by the right brain. Something has impeded the normal physical connection of the hemispheres. The sometimes fantastic conclusions are fitted into an abnormal worldview that make sense to the patient. Then Watzlawick discovered that the same thing happens in people with normal minds or normal problems. The words we use have not only a dictionary meaning but a meaning beyond that. Poetic feelings, ironies, jokes and paradoxes especially have an appeal for some people that they do not have for others. Never explain a joke; we all know that! If the connection doesn't come from within the hearer, logic won't help. The ideas don't fit.

James Fowler, a clinical psychologist, began with the standard models of the process of maturing.[4] We advance from infancy through childhood into adulthood, middle age and the final stages. The final stage is not decrepit old age, but generativity; that is the handing on of life as the mature person has integrated it. Maturity comes slowly by putting together a worldview that satisfies our needs. Over the course of a lifetime the right brain of the mature person of faith has put together a worldview from experiences of daily life, education, belief systems, myths, etcetera. It may not be neat or systematic, but it has a place for everything that the person really believes in, along with a sense of incongruities and a comfortable ignoring of what is not important to the individual, including doubts. Fowler devised tests to measure how and in what circumstances people advanced toward a maturity in faith. He found that a person's worldview changed as he or she progressed through the various rites of passage. He concluded that our worldview amalgamates (1) our values, (2) our power images and (3) our master story.

We are dealing here with psychology, which is a far less "provable" field than the physical sciences. Both Watzlawick and Fowler could be comfortable with a mystery factor that lingered behind their empirical evidence. Perhaps we must also be, but we resist it in our technological age.

4. The Scientific Search for Underpinnings

John Horgan, a senior writer for *Scientific American*, interviewed some forty prominent pure scientists in various fields from astronomy to scientific theology, including evolutionary biology, computer intelligence, complexity theory, cosmology, evolutionary biology, limitology, mathematics, neuroscience, philosophy, physics and social science. He discovered that all these top scientists were searching for some master idea or, as it is sometimes whimsically called, "the single theory of everything," which would unify all sciences. His conclusion was that they were all in despair of finding the ultimate truth. Either they felt that they had reached the end of their search or were in terminal disagreement among themselves. Yet they resisted the necessity of mystery. Hence the name of Horgan's book, *The End of Science: Facing the Limits of Knowledge in the Twilight of the Scientific Age*.[5]

5. Theological Underpinnings

A similar quest occurs in theology. In theology we accept that we have no direct experience of God. The prologue of John's Gospel makes this evident statement.[6] We have never "seen" an incarnation or a trinity. We must attempt a comparison and say that these realities are somewhat like things we know from experience. That is analogy. We cannot prove them. Only revelation and faith spark a connective in us that makes them acceptable. Watzlawick's right hemisphere of the brain is at work. We will see other approaches to the same problem. Once we have the "deposit of faith" as it is called by theologians, then we use logic to systematize our whole understanding and call the results "doctrines" and their study "theology."

In the golden ages of theology we got just so far into the explanations of the concepts of trinity and incarnation, of divine providence and human free will, into the transcendence and immanence of God, etcetera, and then we knew that we were peering back over a fence at the mystery that lay beyond proof.[7] The mystery always beckoned us but was unreachable here. The tree of knowledge was still growing but remained a forbidden fruit. Yet without the mystery life was unbearably dull. The wise sages of the Bible knew this by experience and sensibly praised the God who beckoned but was always unseen, unattainable.

Our worldview—the Where are you coming from?—needed the master story that Fowler has identified to hold it together. This is where rhetoric is so useful. A rhetorical study of wisdom must lead us to mystery. "The beginning of wisdom is the fear of the Lord." Its end is a humble contemplation of what lies so far beyond us that it awes us.

6. The Literary Underpinnings

Karl Rahner has a discussion of metacommunication even though he does not use this word. He distinguished between primordial words and utility words. By utility words Rahner meant the ordinary theological terms with precise meanings. The primordial words have symbolic meanings that reveal the process of becoming; they are never static nor exhausted of meaning. Such, for example, are *spirit, water, night* and *day*. They open into the heart of "the mystery of unity in multiplicity."[8] In effect, they metacommunicate.

For our purposes, Luis Alonso Schökel is more immediately helpful.[9] He simply distinguishes among technical communication, common language and poetry. Workers in all fields from architects to microbiologists develop specific terms and expressions to describe what they are doing. This vocabulary is precise and universally understood. For example, a doctor may state that a patient has a cardiac infarction. The technical word specifies precisely a physical condition that all doctors understand. What the doctor or the patient feels about the situation is of no concern. We all recognize that a difference exists between prose and poetry. A poet may say that a person is dying of a broken heart. That conjures up tragedy or frustration or glorification through suffering, as in the case of Jesus. We supply the meaning besides the words out of our own background of experience.

> *All the world's a stage,*
> *And all the men and women merely players.*
> *They have their exits and their entrances,*
> *And one man in his time plays many parts.*
>   (Shakespeare, *As You Like It,* act II, scene 7, line 139)

Shakespeare used that image of the stage and players several times. He knew that theatergoers found it fitting. They paid the admission price to be able to identify with the characters as the play was acted out. The state-

ment cannot be proved. It is accepted because it fits into
our worldview with our own surplus meanings. As we
used to say in Thomistic philosophy, the argument is *ex
convenientia*; it is "fitting." In English it sounds bad, but
it is realistic even if logically unprovable.

Between technical and poetic language Schökel
placed common speech. Common language is often picturesque. *Reader's Digest* has delighted people for years
with the column "Towards More Picturesque Speech,"
taken from common sayings. "It's better to be known by
six people for something you're proud of than by 60 mil-
lion for something you're not."[10] It appeals because it
invites us to use our imagination.

7. The Power of Metaphor

In formal literary study we may begin with metaphor as a vehicle of expression. Metaphor and all the
derivatives in our litany of figures of speech depend on a
comparison that the hearer or reader makes out of personal understanding beyond the literal sense. "The Lord
is my shepherd." Technically, the Lord is not. Most of us,
however, have enough biblical background to make the
identification in some way even if we have never seen a
shepherd. Although metaphor may be studied either as
a technical mechanism or as an imaginative insight,[11]
it always involves a leap of imagination as the total
worldview bridges the gap between experience and literal meaning. That leap is dependent on the underpinnings that I have attempted to describe above.
Ultimately, the language of wisdom appeals to all
humans because of that creative act of our own.

2

The Character
Formation of a People

1. The Master Story

The books of the Bible that we are discussing fall within the worldwide literature derived from proverbs. Let me repeat that this is the language of the common people.[1] The proverbs of a people form and define the character of the people. To do so they must be inserted within the master story of the people. Biblical proverbs are distinct from those of others because of their worldview. This people had a unique story of how their God had called them to a specific mission in the world, namely, to keep alive his worship and walk in his way.

A master story gives coherence to our life within a community. The community master story must unite the beginning of the story with the projected ending. We never live long enough to write the final chapter of our story, and since the human race still lives on, we need a projection at the end by expectation or prophecy to make it complete. So too, the biblical master story begins with creation in the first book, Genesis (or "beginning"), and ends with the prophecy of how it all ends in the Book of Revelation. Between these bookends the story is one of conflict, confusion, failure and some success by humans and endless compassion and new initiatives by God.

The key theme is the unfailing loving-kindness of God toward a wayward people. "The People" never consists of some exclusive designated community, but rather the whole race. When the story of Genesis reaches the first historically designated man, Abraham, in chapter 12, a promise of blessings for his descendants and through them for all the nations sets the tone of what the whole story shall be. Conflict often rages among the human groups, but with shrewd insight the writers retell the experiences of the people as a conflict from within, using the pattern from the originating story of the Garden of Eden. Sin seems to overwhelm the human actors, but they are always rescued by the mercy of a God who punishes and yet forgives, who gives death but also a new life.

The Exodus from Egypt becomes the governing model of this theme. Between Abraham, the first believer in a unique Yahweh, and Moses, the liberator, the family of believers almost vanishes as a community except for a tenuous memory of an initiating promise. Moses, more Egyptian than Israelite, needs to rediscover both the traditional faith and promise. Then he must endure the apparent failure of his own leadership and the sharp disillusionment of his people. Yet even at the lowest points, God always brings them back ecstatically or painfully to their mission.

The Jesus story, interpreted so often in the New Testament as a new Exodus, reveals the same theme. By his day, the Jewish people had finally achieved practical worship of God and become satisfied with their mission. The historical Jesus, the Messiah and the only-begotten God, led them across the sea of complacency to a new mission to all peoples. The historical Jesus seems to end in failure, abandoned and discredited as a criminal, but actually he turns out to be the bringer of salvation to all who believe in him. The Christian community is on its way to the predicted manifestation of the power and glory of God who saves. To make sense, the whole story must be accepted.

Generation after generation had handed down the master story by word of mouth. Most of the Israelites were born into this tradition, but many others became converts as the centuries went by.[2] Genealogical descent was not a requirement, although they valued genealogies. Pagans were not excluded,[3] but all members learned either from their parents and clan elders or from the neighbors they met. Such is the usual way of education. The parents also learned more and became better teachers as they advanced through life and persevered, as Fowler discovered. Most of all, they learned that fidelity was a mutual virtue expected of both Yahweh and the chosen people.

Thus the wisdom books are uniquely Jewish, even when repeating secular proverbs or taking off from them. The "family values" expressed are the values of the Lord. The Book of Proverbs can mimic the Egyptian sayings of a famous sage, Amen-em-ope, or quote Agur, a pagan.[4] The Book of Job is set in a non-Israelite background. Jonah the Jewish prophet is an ironic character sketched against the background of the pagan Ninevites who repented. And yet the orientation was entirely different. This people worshiped only one God and had only one Temple. Their code of living meant something different even when they acted externally in the same way. They were recognized as distinct by their neighbors and were often derided for their uniqueness.[5]

2. The Handing On of the Tradition

We do not know much about early Israelite education. What we do know confirms the expectation that it began in the home. The Book of Proverbs frequently has a father or mother addressing "my son."[6] The "son" is a generic term for young learners, not for any particular son.

Later, when the monarchy had been established, the need for formal education to fill government posts from diplomats to tax collectors demanded some knowledge of international languages and customs, management techniques, and basic mathematics, etcetera.[7] Proverbs 25:1 names the collectors of the section that follows: "These also are proverbs of Solomon. The men of Hezekiah, king of Judah, transmitted them." It exemplifies the sophistication of educated men of that era. Proverbs and other wisdom sayings are frequently attributed to Solomon as the preeminent wise man, but the authority of the king as legislator is never invoked.[8] The Temple functionaries apparently were also educated men. The widely understood source for much of the material in the Pentateuch, the so-called priestly document, has been proposed as a sample of priestly teaching for young children in the Temple. They could more easily memorize it because of its numerical schemes and genealogies. Some of the priestly passages, and perhaps the Deuteronomic materials as well, are similar to the wisdom tradition. In addition to these, some prophetic books, notably Isaiah and Amos, also have sections that we label as creation wisdom.

We have sometimes referred to the whole of the Old Testament as Torah, although we know the traditional three-part division into the Law, the former and later Prophets and the Writings. Translating Torah as the

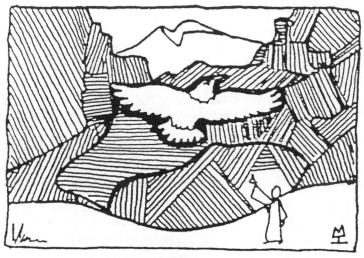

"Does the eagle soar at your command?"
Job 39:27

Law, however, can be misleading.[9] *Law* to contemporary Americans conjures up pictures of legislators, judicial systems and a police force. The center of Torah (which means "instruction") is the story. Torah ethics does exist but not as a legal code in our understanding. Torah exists as the master story of a people of God sent on a mission to worship him and to make him known to the nations.[10] The consoling thing to the nations is that Israel failed so miserably in the mission but still retained its distinctiveness as the chosen people. In an odd way Israel could not forget God's fidelity even when it tried to forget its own obligation toward him. The Old Testament story cries aloud for salvation, not for acclamation of superiority or victory. The story had appeal to others precisely because it did embody a hope for a savior.

3. How Wisdom Builds Character Formation

To have such far-reaching consequences, the proverbial way of speaking requires two things: (1) that the proverb maker and the hearer share some nucleus of the master story that forms a worldview; (2) that the proverb maker leave room for the hearer to make connections out of personal experience and wisdom.

All the specific applications of wisdom are seen against that unique faith of Israel which was told in story beginning with the creation of the world, the call of Abraham, the deliverance under Moses and the founding of a monarchy doomed to failure from the beginning. "All the ways of a man may be pure in his own eyes, but it is the LORD who proves the spirit" (Prov 16:2).[11]

In a way this may correspond to what we call the right of individual conscience. As Christians we take this for granted. The conscience, however, must be an informed conscience. Most of all it must be informed by the story. To the teacher of proverbs the sayings represented the mature advice of the elders.[12] The teachings were directive but not imposed. One could walk in that way with considerable forgiveness for deviations, or one could leave the assembly. The proverb maker left lots of room for the hearer to make the connections between the advice and one's personal experience.

4. The Maturing of the Teachers

Proverbs provided a basic direction of attitudes toward communal living for the individual and thus built up the corporate character. They were not rules imposed by legal authority but clear suggestions regarding how one was expected to act in the community. Like the later so-called legal dispensations, they were embodied within the master story of the Israelite people.

As noted previously, Fowler studied individuals for growth in faith maturing. Perhaps we can posit a similar process in social groups. The common wisdom of the Bible began with the master story of the myths of creation, which were then adapted to the later covenant relationship with Abraham. It moved from the slim theology of the patriarchal age to the Mosaic requirements and on to the later written commandments, prescripts and such. It took many centuries to get beyond adolescence.

> *I mean that as long as the heir is not of age, he is no different from a slave, although he is the owner of everything, but he is under the supervision of guardians and administrators until the date set by his father. In the same way we also, when we were not of age, were enslaved to the elemental powers of the world.* (Gal 4:1–3)

The adolescence of Israel involved them in the experiment of monarchy, its disastrous end and the reconstruction of the savior myth in the postexilic period.

5. The Change of Worldview in the Later Wisdom

Over the ages, as the people's wisdom came to be written down and polished by more sophisticated writers, it came to invade prophetic sayings, essays and stories. The worldview of the writers was changing with the centuries. The central part of the Book of Proverbs probably represents a miscellaneous collection of early proverbs, while the writing of Ben Sirach in the second century B.C. represents a much later stage of studied Judaism that centered on Torah. In turn, the Wisdom of Solomon in the first century B.C. was an adaptation to the understandings of the Jewish Dispersion in a Hellenistic world.

The postexilic era from 540 B.C. to the time of Jesus is most interesting, comparable to the middle-age crisis in most of our lives. Judaism after the Babylonian Captivity reconstructed its older ethos in such wisdom writings as Job, Qoheleth and Jonah. These writers had the courage to grapple with what were for them the insoluble problems from the earlier tradition. Job addresses the problem of the just man who is punished, and Qoheleth tackles the opposite problem of the vanity of undeserved success. Job violently accuses God of acting unjustly in depriving him of all good but is admired by God for being a man and has it all restored. Qoheleth has everything and finds it all boring except that to eat, drink and be merry should be enjoyed fully as a gift of God. Jonah is the only preacher in the Bible who leads a whole pagan city to repentance but is angered because he doesn't get to see the sinners smitten by God's wrath. Irony and paradox rules all these books. And wit invades them all as well, for when life becomes unbearable, only a touch of humor gives the reader an outlet.

6. The Role of Myth in Our Thinking

Myth in the Israelite sense always exercised its influence. At the base of society's worldviews lay some fragments or whole blocks of myth. As Fowler concluded, myth is a most important dynamic in personal master stories. But it is just as true that whole societies live on master stories which attempt to explain life. They have power even today. A recent survey showed that 83 percent of the American public believe in heaven, but in a secular culture such as ours, we know, of course, that no real evidence exists that can prove such beliefs. Joseph Campbell has identified a common plot of myths from all over the world that he calls the monomyth.[13] The monomyth is a story of the hero who comes from outside, sometimes secretly, dies and rises and so opens the way to salvation and life for others. This is the myth of creation and redemption, the worldview in which all wisdom is situated. The Hebrew Bible is full of it and so is our New Testament.

3

The Proverb as
Fundamental Wisdom

1. Some Shrewd Proverbs from the Bible

Having pried into their hidden presuppositions and purposes, let us come face to face with some proverbs. A shrewdness pervades many of these observations on human experience and we recognize them still.

> *Who scream? Who shriek?*
> *Who have strife? Who have anxiety?*
> *Who have wounds for nothing?*
> *Who have black eyes?*
> *Those who linger long over wine,*
> *those who engage in trials of blended wine.*
> (Prov 23:29–30)

We know how alcohol still creates this very scene!

> *"Bad, bad!" says the buyer;*
> *but once he has gone his way, he boasts.*
> (Prov 20:14)

Any shopping spree today can produce the same comment. You should hear the deal I worked out on my new car!

> *Like a crazed archer*
> > *scattering firebrands and deadly arrows*
> *Is the man who deceives his neighbor,*
> > *and then says, "I was only joking."* (Prov 26:18–19)

What about the man who tries to set our house on fire and then says, "I was only joking"? We want to sue him for that.

> *The laborer's appetite labors for him,*
> > *for his mouth urges him on.* (Prov 16:26)

Even today we recognize that the best incentive to work is that we are getting hungry.

> *A man who has a bribe to offer rates it a magic stone;*
> > *at every turn it brings him success.* (Prov 17:8)

Our newspapers today are full of stories of people who bribe their way to influence—until they are caught. What else is new in politics?

Not all proverbs, of course, have this flair for wit. Many of them are platitudinous common sense, but not the less valuable.

> *The just man takes care of his beast,*
> > *but the heart of the wicked is merciless.* (Prov 12:10)

> *Complete your outdoor tasks,*
> > *and arrange your work in the field;*
> > *afterward you can establish your house.* (Prov 24:27)

> *One man is lavish yet grows still richer;*
> > *another is too sparing, yet is the poorer.* (Prov 11:24)

Sometimes the people's sayings can be downright cutting.

A worthy wife is the crown of her husband,
but a disgraceful one is like rot in his bones.
(Prov 12:4)

The foolish son is ruin to his father,
and the nagging of a wife is a persistent leak.
(Prov 19:13)

How many of the approximately nine hundred verses in the Book of Proverbs should be considered witty in one way or another is a subjective decision, of course. I would consider some 10 percent a solid estimate for myself. However, it takes only a little salt to season the soup.

2. The Function of Proverbs

In both the biblical and contemporary languages, the word *proverb* has a very extensive range of meanings. A proverb may mean a short, pithy saying about experience (which is its more common meaning), a riddle, a parable or a story with wit, and perhaps other things as well. As quoted in the introduction, no one has ever devised the proverb that explains what a proverb is. They are called proverbs by collectors today simply because people call them proverbs. If we begin by accepting proverbs as one way in which the common people speak, we can perhaps sense more of what they were saying to one another. The birthing place of wisdom is the proverb.

Discerning the function of proverbs in common speech seems to me to offer an opportunity to gain more insight into our contemporary understanding of the mysteries of our faith. The people handed down the faith by the same process that gave birth to wisdom, namely, by interpreting their worldview in the light of their experiences.

It is agreed that proverbs are the basic building blocks of wisdom and that they come eventually from the hard-earned experience of family or clan. Why do people create and then collect proverbs? What use are they to society?

> *Very soon he will be dead; so he says, "Let me eat up all I*
> *   have."*
> *Soon he will be well; so he says, "Let me economize."*

That one is Akkadian from about three thousand years ago.[1]

> *A lazy man is no better than a dead one;*
> *   but he takes up more room.*

That one is from Alabama.[2] We instinctively figure out the contrast in the cost of laziness.

> *As vinegar to the teeth, and smoke to the eyes,*
> *   is the sluggard to those who use him as a messenger.*

That is from Proverbs 10:26.

You will note a certain wry humor here. Why do we cite Murphy's Law: "If anything can go wrong, it will?" Who Murphy was is irrelevant to us; it is simply a clever truth. Jesus said to Peter, "When you were younger, you used to dress yourself and go where you wanted; but when you grow old, you will stretch out your hands, and someone else will dress you and lead you where you do not want to go" (John 21:18). Jesus basically repeats a saying of the people, that is, a proverb. In my religious

"Oh that my words were written down"
Job 19:23

community the version is: "You know you are retired
when they ask you for the car keys."

What function do such sayings have rhetorically?
They don't prove anything; they are only a thin slice of
experience. Proverbs are not general principles and certainly not rules. All told, however, they form a kind of
survivor's manual. As with Murphy's Law, when everything keeps going wrong, at least we know that this is
normal. Their clever rhetoric aims to persuade us to
action–or even to inaction, if it is the virtue of patience
that is needed. In that sense all proverbial rhetoric is
formative. But how does this make an appeal to us–at
least, to some of us at some times?

3. Making Sense out of Proverbs

Let me try to illustrate how my presuppositions work out rhetorically in the sayings about the sluggard in the Book of Proverbs. All the sayings about the lazy man are noted below.

> *Go to the ant, O sluggard,*
> > *study her ways and learn wisdom;* (Prov 6:6)

> *How long, O sluggard, will you rest?*
> > *when will you rise from your sleep?* (Prov 6:9)

> *As vinegar to the teeth, and smoke to the eyes,*
> > *is the sluggard to those who use him as a messenger.*
> > > (Prov 10:26)

> *The soul of the sluggard craves in vain,*
> > *but the diligent soul is amply satisfied.* (Prov 13:4)

> *Laziness plunges a man into deep sleep,*
> > *and the sluggard must go hungry.* (Prov 19:15)

> *The sluggard loses his hand in the dish;*
> > *he will not even lift it to his mouth.* (Prov 19:24)

> *In seedtime the sluggard plows not;*
> > *when he looks for the harvest, it is not there.*
> > > (Prov 20:4)

> *I passed by the field of the sluggard,*
> > *by the vineyard of the man without sense;*
> *And behold! it was all overgrown with thistles;*
> > *its surface was covered with nettles,*
> > *and its stone wall broken down.*
> *And as I gazed at it, I reflected;*
> > *I saw and learned the lesson:*

A little sleep, a little slumber,
  a little folding of the arms to rest—
Then will poverty come upon you like a highwayman,
  and want like an armed man. (Prov 24:30–34)

The sluggard says, "There is a lion in the street,
  a lion in the middle of the square!"
The door turns on its hinges,
  the sluggard, on his bed!
The sluggard loses his hand in the dish;
  he is too weary to lift it to his mouth.
The sluggard imagines himself wiser
  than seven men who answer with good sense.
                                (Prov 26:13–16)

All of these verses seem to be correctly translated in the New American Bible version and have no great textual problems.[3]

First of all, the English printed text which we read immediately suggests that this is poetry, but that may be due simply to the modern typesetter. The original was not handwritten in poetic blocks of text.[4] But whether one thinks this was originally poetic or not, we immediately notice that the first line makes a statement and usually the second or following lines line completes it or perhaps reverses the picture. We call it complementary or antithetical parallelism, but it is not always neat. The thought though has a certain rhythm to it.

The earliest formulations of proverbs seem to have existed as sayings within the family or clan. Perhaps the wording and format were somewhat different, but the basic comment was the "there." We cannot tie down a precise social setting for every proverb. No one group is identified; the sluggard may be a farmer or a merchant or a gourmet or even a messenger. The observations have been derived from multiple sightings even if focused on a narrow subject. In general, however, the sayings are all shrewd observations of character.

4. The Flavoring of Wit in Proverbs

The shrewdness of proverbs often takes the form of wit. Wit is the art of gracious speech.[5] Quintillian, the rhetorician of Latin literature, insisted that "wit is a form of repartee which exhibits mental agility and linguistic grace." Hazlitt, the English literary critic, said wit is the product of art and fantasy and that the incongruous "is the essence of comedy." Kierkegaard, the philosopher, wrote, "...wherever there is contradiction, the comical is present."

Why did proverbs appeal in their oral form (and even in written form) to the people? Because they have wit for those who are witty.[6] But where did the witty find the odd connections in these pictures? First, they collected all those images—the vinegar that sets teeth on edge, the smoke blown in the eyes (we still use that one), the lazy rising from sleep, the dish and the sluggish hand, the barren field at harvest time, the vineyard overgrown with thistles, the folding of the hands with a sigh, the highwayman, the lion in the street, the door swinging on its hinges and so on. Yet even when people observed these actions, why did they find the connection with the sluggard so wise and fitting that they then preserved the sayings so carefully?

The Bible is not alone in this touch of wit. Proverbs in all cultures tend to have a seasoning of humor about them. In the nine quotations about the sluggard in Proverbs the first is a neutral observation, three are platitudes and five are witty.[7] As a comparison, if one opens the standard *American Proverbs* to "lazy," there are ten listings with a provenance for each:

1. *The lazy man always finds excuses. Ala., Ga.*
2. *A lazy man is no better than a dead one, but he takes up more room. Ala., Ga.*
3. *A lazy man will live the longest. Ont.*
4. *A lazy man works the hardest. N.Y., S.C.*
5. *A lazy person will never try to see the light. Calif.*
6. *Lazy folks are most efficient. Ont.*
7. *Lazy folks' stomachs don't get tired. Ont.*
8. *The lazy man goes to his work like a thief to the gallows. Wis.*
9. *The lazy man takes the most pain. W.Va.*
10. *A man who can't get up to loaf is too lazy to enjoy it. Ala., Ga.*[8]

The proportion of witty sayings here is about the same as it is for proverbs. A reversal of judgment is often involved. The sluggard thinks he is smart in making a living by running errands for clever patrons. He does the dirty work of delivering messages that set the recipients' teeth on edge like vinegar and blow smoke in their eyes. He is being used, and is a laughingstock to the clever.[9] "As vinegar to the teeth, and smoke to the eyes, is the sluggard to those who use him as a messenger" (Prov 10:26). The Greek comic dramatists used that kind of a character in their plays to get a laugh because he boasts himself above his station but is revealed at the end as hollow. That is one of our own favorite plots for comedy.

5. The Hidden Subsurface of Humor

Any literary image works by substituting an easily envisioned concrete situation for an abstraction. The connection that the metaphor implies is made by the hearer or reader. A response is called for. The response comes from an implied worldview. The observations about the lazy man pertain to the world of work. The hearer or reader needs to connect them to one's own work ethic, otherwise nothing humorous is seen. The American proverb from Alabama quoted above reads:

> A *lazy man is no better than a dead one, but he takes up more room.*

That seems to spring from our own work ethic, which measures a person's worth on an economic basis. In contrast the examples cited from the Book of Proverbs say:

> *The sluggard says, "There is a lion in the street,*
>   *a lion in the middle of the square!"*
> *The door turns on its hinges,*
>   *the sluggard, on his bed!*
> *The sluggard loses his hand in the dish;*
>   *he is too weary to lift it to his mouth.*
> *The sluggard imagines himself wiser*
>   *than seven men who answer with good sense.*
> (Prov 26:13–16)

These imply that the lazy man is measured by his lack of wisdom. That is a different viewpoint.

What was the world viewpoint behind the biblical proverb?

Honest work was certainly expected from those who belonged to this Israelite family or clan. But the sluggard was ridiculed for having an unwise and unacceptable lifestyle because the people needed to preserve the land of Israel, which the Lord had given them. Ridicule is a common way in which a society enforces order. This ridicule, however, is gentle.[10] It pokes fun at the fool but imposes no penalty beyond that.

6. The Bible's Worldview

And what is behind the Bible's work ethic? Achievement? Wealth? Power? A larger worldview emerges when we ask why these sayings were included in the Book of Proverbs which was eventually canonized by the people as the word of God. No law of Moses is adduced, no stories from the public history, no voice of prophet or priest. The master story of the Hebrews, however, always made them conscious that as the people of God they had a mission. That mission affected their feet, not just their heads. They must walk in the way of the Lord. To be a member of this People one had to use one's talents for the good of all. Simply sleeping away the days would not do. That worldview needs to be shared by both the ancient and contemporary readers. If not, the proverbs have no sting and perhaps make little sense.

Similar statements can be found in other ancient literature, but the worldview is different. The master story of this clan began with the stately and ordered procession of the seven days of creation as now recorded in Genesis 1. Whether the story was written before or after these early proverbs were popular makes little difference. The tradition was ready to accept both versions. In the mythologically phrased story in Genesis the living creatures were climaxed by the created images of God, male and female humans. They were commissioned to fill the earth and subdue it and to have dominion over all the living things that move on the earth (Gen 1:28). Then on the last day God rested and let his creatures take over. In the second story of paradise the man was condemned to eat his bread in toil and by the sweat of his brow (Gen 3:17). That was how life went and that was the order God had imposed. The Hebrews could not forget where their master story began.

7. Are the Proverbs Religious?

It may be said that these sayings about the sluggard are secular. On the surface that is true. Often no mention is made of the Lord.[11] When it is, one can notice how the entrance of the Lord changes the picture, often toward paradox.

> *My son, forget not my teaching,*
> *keep in mind my commands;*
> *For many days, and years of life,*
> *and peace, will they bring you.*
> *Let not kindness and fidelity leave you;*
> *bind them around your neck;*
> *Then will you win favor and good esteem*
> *before God and man.*
> *Trust in the LORD with all your heart,*
> *on your own intelligence rely not;*
> *In all your ways be mindful of him,*
> *and he will make straight your paths.*
> *Be not wise in your own eyes,*
> *fear the LORD and turn away from evil;*
> *This will mean health for your flesh*
> *and vigor for your bones.*
> *Honor the LORD with your wealth,*
> *with first fruits of all your produce;*
> *Then will your barns be filled with grain,*
> *with new wine your vats will overflow.*
> *The discipline of the LORD, my son, disdain not;*
> *spurn not his reproof;*

> *For whom the* LORD *loves he reproves*
> *and chastises the son he favors.* (Prov 3:1–12)

The poem praises wisdom that comes from the Lord through the teaching of the father. Many good things are promised to the son who respects the Lord and practices fidelity, kindness and humility. But then the last line turns this upside down and promises chastisement to the son whom the Lord loves. The whole expected theology of retribution now runs in reverse.

8. Conclusion

The rhetoric of paradox requires seeing both sides of the picture and is often beyond the understanding of one who does not know the whole story. The fascination with the sluggard is a small example of how the common people responded to the frustrations of life understood religiously as the chastisement of the son the Lord loves. The people's proverbs met the incongruities of life with wit and made life bearable. Behind the chuckle was an unbreakable faith of the true people of God that the Lord would always take care of them. They accepted these flexible insights into how to live and thus survived. Proverbs preserved good order and good humor.

4

The Playful Proverb

1. The Function of Proverbs for Young and Old

The keynote poem at the beginning of the Book of Proverbs outlines the function of proverbs.

The Proverbs of Solomon, the son of David,
*   king of Israel:*
That men may appreciate wisdom and discipline,
*   may understand words of intelligence;*
May receive training in wise conduct,
*   in what is right, just and honest;*
That resourcefulness may be imparted to the simple,
*   to the young man knowledge and discretion.*
A wise man by hearing them will advance in learning,
*   an intelligent man will gain sound guidance,*
That he may comprehend proverb and parable,
*   the words of the wise and their riddle.*
The fear of the LORD *is the beginning of knowledge;*
*   wisdom and instruction fools despise.* (Prov 1:1–7)

The function of proverbs is to enable all of us to appreciate wisdom. *Wisdom* is described as discipline, intelligence, wise conduct, resourcefulness, knowledge, discretion, guidance. It is not a simple quality. Nor is proverb the only form of a saying. We have proverbs and parable, words of the wise and riddles.[1]

The last poem in the Book of Proverbs pictures the "worthy wife" as the epitome of wisdom. It ends:

> *Charm is deceptive and beauty fleeting;*
>   *the woman who fears the LORD is to be praised.*
> (Prov 31:30)

The later editors who crafted these first and last poems clearly saw them as bookends to what Proverbs was about.[2] They are not notably proverbial in style if one defines a proverb narrowly.[3] Yet the people called the whole collection a book of proverbs. However sophisticated the later editors and contributors may have been, the thought and language came from the folk.

First of all, one puzzles over "the fear of the Lord." In our language and social context "fear of the Lord" is a dreadful way of beginning anything. In biblical language, however, the "fear of the Lord" more often than not should be translated as awe at the power and wisdom and kindliness of the Lord displayed to us.[4] Isaiah pictured the savior who will come into the world in these words:

> *The spirit of the LORD shall rest upon him:*
>   *a spirit of wisdom and of understanding,*
> *A spirit of counsel and of strength,*
>   *a spirit of knowledge and of fear of the LORD,*
> *and his delight shall be the fear of the LORD.*
> (Isa 11:2–3)

The fear of the Lord is a God-given spirit that enlightens and enlivens as the hope of a savior demanded. It is a delight.

3. Parents as Teachers

The wise man and woman begins the teaching of the young at home.

> *Hear, my son, your father's instruction,*
> *and reject not your mother's teaching;* (Prov 1:8)

The "son" is, of course, generic. Both the father and the mother are the teachers.[5] They are the most important molders of character for the young.[6] Having noted that, we also note the masculine tone of what follows. At first, the sayings seem disconnected, but they soon marshal themselves around the theme of adultery and faithful love of a wife. The prophets sometimes used that image to picture the relationship between Yahweh and Israel, relating either to rejection or fidelity in love.[7] Such was the great commandment of the Law. It was also the point of the master story in which it was embedded.

By chapter 5 the father as teacher is giving some hardheaded warnings to his son about fidelity in marriage.

> *The lips of an adulteress drip with honey,*
> *and her mouth is smoother than oil;*
> *But in the end she is as bitter as wormwood,*
> *as sharp as a two-edged sword.* (Prov 5:3–4)

The father's advice begins to sound like hard-won experience:

> *And I saw among the simple ones,*
> *I observed among the young men,*
> *a youth with no sense,*
> *Going along the street near the corner,*
> *then walking in the direction of her house—*

"Throw stones at birds and you scare them away"
Sirach 22:20

In the twilight, at dusk of day,
  at the time of the dark of night.
And lo! the woman comes to meet him,
  robed like a harlot, with secret designs—
She is fickle and unruly,
  in her home her feet cannot rest;
Now she is in the streets, now in the open squares,
  and at every corner she lurks in ambush—
When she seizes him, she kisses him,
  and with an impudent look says to him:
"...Come, let us drink our fill of love,
  until morning, let us feast on love!
For my husband is not at home,
  he has gone on a long journey;
A bag of money he took with him,
  not till the full moon will he return home."
She wins him over by her repeated urging,
  with her smooth lips she leads him astray;

> *He follows her stupidly,*
>   *like an ox that is led to slaughter;*
> *Her house is made up of ways to the nether world,*
>   *leading down into the chambers of death.*
>   (Prov 7:7–13, 18–22, 27)

The advice is rambling but hooks into a picture he had described before.

> *For vindictive is the husband's wrath,*
>   *he will have no pity on the day of vengeance;*
> *He will not consider any restitution,*
>   *nor be satisfied with the greatest gifts.* (Prov 6:34–35)

That needs no commentary. It is not only observably true; it is witty. Will its wit resonate in the reader?

However, the wise father also knows the beauty of true love and he paints a charming picture of it:

> *Drink water from your own cistern,*
>   *running water from your own well.*
> *…Let your fountain be yours alone,*
>   *not one shared with strangers;*
> *And have joy of the wife of your youth,*
>   *your lovely hind, your graceful doe.*
> *Her love will invigorate you always,*
>   *through her love you will flourish continually,*
> *Why then, my son, should you go astray for another's wife*
>   *and accept the embraces of an adulteress?*
> *…When you lie down she will watch over you,*
>   *and when you wake, she will share your concerns;*
>   *wherever you turn, she will guide you.*
>   (Prov 5:15, 17–19, 22, 20)

4. The Ascent to Higher Wisdom

The youth learns the truth about the wisdom of sex from the experience of the father. When the Wise Man then ventures to gaze beyond the earthy experience of the faithful wife, he can leap into the heavens for the archetype of wisdom. He can hear this feminine voice of life speaking of life to him.

> *"The* LORD *begot me, the first-born of his ways,*
>   *the forerunner of his prodigies of long ago;*
> *From of old I was poured forth,*
>   *at the first, before the earth.*
> *While as yet the earth and the fields were not made,*
>   *nor the first clods of the world."*
> *"When he established the heavens I was there,*
>   *when he marked out the vault over the face of the deep;*
> *Then was I beside him as his craftsman,*
>   *and I was his delight day by day,*
> *Playing before him all the while,*
>   *playing on the surface of his earth;*
>   *and I found delight in the sons of men...."*
>
>   (Prov 8:22–23, 26–27, 30–31)

We have soared from the barroom to the light of the heavens at creation.[8]

How did the writer know this? No mention is made of vision or revelation. The person who wrote it was presumably a married man. He knew the joys of a happy married life with the woman he loved. Yet his wife was the lifegiver in so many more ways than himself. And she knew far more than he. Such wisdom, he concluded, must have been there from the beginning. The Woman was ascending to play before the Creator God and yet descending to delight among us. Jesus was later to say much the same of himself.[9]

5. Lady Wisdom and Woman Folly

Watzlawick's metacommunication is at work here. The section began with a barroom contrast between adultery and fidelity—and a chuckle. The ending of the instruction in chapter 9 makes a sharp antithesis between Lady Wisdom and the Woman Folly. Both have prepared a banquet and both have called to the simple Israelite. The true characters of these women are delineated through in what happens to those who follow each. The true believer knows Lady Wisdom in the daily rounds of pious life. The woman Folly belongs to the pagans in their rituals of the fertility goddess:

> *Wisdom has built her house,*
> > *she has set up her seven columns;*
> *She has dressed her meat, mixed her wine,*
> > *yes, she has spread her table.*
> *She has sent out her maidens; she calls*
> > *from the heights out over the city:*
> *"Let whoever is simple turn in here;*
> > *to him who lacks understanding, I say,*
> *Come, eat of my food,*
> > *and drink of the wine I have mixed!"* (Prov 9:1–5)

> *The woman Folly is fickle,*
> > *she is inane, and knows nothing.*
> *She sits at the door of her house*
> > *upon a seat on the city heights,*
> *Calling to passers-by*
> > *as they go on their straight way:*
> *"Let whoever is simple turn in here,*
> > *or who lacks understanding; for to him I say,*
> *Stolen water is sweet,*
> > *and bread gotten secretly is pleasing!"*

> *Little he knows that the shades are there,*
> *that in the depths of the nether world are her guests!*
> (Prov 9:13–18)

The pictures describe what one can sink to or the sublime that one can rise to. Paradoxes are something of a game of serious playfulness.

6. The Early Proverbs

The collections of early proverbs as we more usually think of such collections begin with chapter 10:

> *The Proverbs of Solomon:*
> *A wise son makes his father glad,*
> *but a foolish son is a grief to his mother.* (Prov 10:1)

These may or may not be the sayings of Solomon. A later entry in the text notes:

> *These also are proverbs of Solomon. The men of*
> *Hezekiah, king of Judah, transmitted them.*
> (Prov 25:1)

As with most collections of proverbs, not much order exists. Occasionally a few sayings on the same subject are connected, such as those about laziness, honest speech, respect for others' rights and so on.[10] Sometimes we have a series of proverbs that begins with the same words, such as "better than." This does not help us much to savor the meaning.

A smaller collection at Proverbs 22:17—24:22 comes from an Egyptian source.

> *That your trust may be in the LORD,*
> *I make known to you the words of Amen-em-Ope.*
> (Prov 22:19)

We have the writing of Amen-em-ope on a papyrus scroll in Egypt dating between the seventh and sixth century B.C.[11] He seems to have been a civil servant who was giving advice to his son on how to succeed in government. The Bible does not copy Amen-em-ope but parallels his sayings with Israelite versions for trainees in government service.

7. The Ending of the Book

After twenty chapters of these unconnected proverbs, a curious collection of short non-Israelite sayings follows. Most interesting are the words of Agur, son of Jakeh the Massaite:

> *The pronouncement of mortal man: "I am not God;*
> *I am not God, that I should prevail.*
> *Why, I am the most stupid of men,*
> *and have not even human intelligence;*
> *Neither have I learned wisdom,*
> *nor have I the knowledge of the Holy One.*
> *Who has gone up to heaven and come down again—*
> *who has cupped the wind in his hands?*
> *Who has bound up the waters in a cloak—*
> *who has marked out all the ends of the earth?*
> *What is his name, what is his son's name,*
> *if you know it?"*
> *Every word of God is tested;*
> *he is a shield to those who take refuge in him.*
> *Add nothing to his words,*
> *lest he reprove you, and you be exposed as a deceiver.*
> (Prov 30:1–6)

The pagan sage, a Massaite, knows the problem of being a truly wise man. To have true wisdom one would need to be above the world and see all that is happening. The proverbs of the wise are narrow slices of experience, not universal principles. Jesus later says to Nicodemus that he is the one who has come down from heaven with such wisdom (John 3:13). The task is awesome. One can only accept every word of God and add nothing to it.

Then to illustrate that the riddles mentioned in the opening poem are truly a part of proverbs, chapter 30:7–33 contains a litany of riddles that are characteristic of all generations. The game is to connect what unites these things—the metacommunication approach.

> *Three things are too wonderful for me,*
> *yes, four I cannot understand:*
> *The way of an eagle in the air,*
> *the way of a serpent upon a rock,*
> *The way of a ship on the high seas,*
> *and the way of a man with a maiden.* (Prov 30:18–19)

Finally, we have the shrewd words of another Massaite:

> The words of Lemuel, king of Massa. The advice which his mother gave him:

> *What, my son, my first-born!*
> *what, O son of my womb;*
> *what, O son of my vows!*
> *Give not your vigor to women,*
> *nor your strength to those who ruin kings.*
> *It is not for kings, O Lemuel,*
> *not for kings to drink wine;*
> *strong drink is not for princes!*
> *Lest in drinking they forget what the law decrees,*
> *and violate the rights of all who are in need.*
> (Prov 31:1–5)

8. The Closing Poem

As mentioned, the opening poem is matched by one at the end. The search for wisdom in the first nine chapters had ended with Lady Wisdom playing before the God of creation and "her delight was to be with the sons of men." Now the "worthy wife" delights in her role as the wise woman.

> *When one finds a worthy wife,*
> *her value is far beyond pearls.*
> *Her husband, entrusting his heart to her,*
> *has an unfailing prize.*
> *She brings him good, and not evil,*
> *all the days of her life.*
> *She obtains wool and flax*
> *and makes cloth with skillful hands.*
> *Like merchant ships,*
> *she secures her provisions from afar.*
> *She rises while it is still night,*
> *and distributes food to her household.*
> *She picks out a field to purchase;*
> *out of her earnings she plants a vineyard.*
> *She is girt about with strength,*
> *and sturdy are her arms.*
> *She enjoys the success of her dealings;*
> *at night her lamp is undimmed.*
> *She puts her hands to the distaff,*
> *and her fingers ply the spindle.*
> *She reaches out her hands to the poor,*
> *and extends her arms to the needy.*
> *She fears not the snow for her household;*
> *all her charges are doubly clothed.*
> *She makes her own coverlets;*
> *fine linen and purple are her clothing.*
> *Her husband is prominent at the city gates*
> *as he sits with the elders of the land.*

She makes garments and sells them,
  and stocks the merchants with belts.
She is clothed with strength and dignity,
  and she laughs at the days to come.
She opens her mouth in wisdom,
  and on her tongue is kindly counsel.
She watches the conduct of her household,
  and eats not her food in idleness.
Her children rise up and praise her;
  her husband, too, extols her:
"Many are the women of proven worth,
  but you have excelled them all."
Charm is deceptive and beauty fleeting;
  the woman who fears the LORD is to be praised.
Give her a reward of her labors,
  and let her works praise her at the city gates.
                                    (Prov 31:10–31)

This is the experience of Lady Wisdom in a house dress, idealized perhaps, but very real. The same pattern of contrast between adultery and fidelity operates here as in Proverbs 5—8. The insight does not soar so high, but it is a noble picture. Her greatest praise is that she stands in awe of the goodness of the Lord whom she tries to imitate.

9. A Summing Up

The problem with Lady Wisdom is not where she came from, but what she is doing now. Discovering another local myth as the source will not settle the question. The question in rhetoric is how these pictures were drawn to persuade the readers then and now to seek wisdom and to act on it. The appeal was to something that already existed within the reader. For the true Israelite it was a broad tradition and a worldview inspired by faith. To those who had this faith the images were endlessly adaptable and imaginative.[12] If the technical problems of source were solved, Lady Wisdom would lose her appeal. So would the Mona Lisa, if she lost her smile.

The intricate workings of our whole self as it interprets data and comfortably finds an appropriate place for it is a grace of God. Yet the choice and sound of the words is also gracious. Like Wisdom herself it must delight to be with us. The Creator God is still playing among these sons and daughters and their children. Wisdom is his delight.

5

The Irascible Job

1. The Prologue

The Book of Job opens with a short story. Both we and ancient listeners know what kind of story it is. Job lived in the timeless land of Uz "somewhere over the rainbow," as we might say.[1] The indefiniteness introduces us to a universal plot. Job is described as an unbelievably blameless man. He is rich beyond hope, a respected family man, concerned to offer sacrifice lest his children may have sinned by enjoying life too much. Then the Satan enters as the inspector general to uncover his one flaw.

> One day, when the sons of God came to present themselves before the LORD, Satan also came among them. And the Lord said to Satan, "Whence do you come?" Then Satan answered the LORD and said, "From roaming the earth and patrolling it."
> (Job 1:6–7)

This patrolling Satan is an unknown character to the Israelite tradition but one comfortable to pagan imaginings.[2] However, he is also at home with us, for in most people's own stories, we all suspect that some evil one is watching to entrap us.

The hypothetical problem emerges for the readers to ponder. Satan challenges the Lord that he can seduce Job away from his perfect ways. He gets the Lord's permission to destroy everything that Job has: wealth, family, reputation. Job is left lying prostrate on the ground but still saying piously:

> *Naked I came forth from my mother's womb,*
> *And naked shall I go back again.*
> *The Lord gabe the Lord has taken away:*
> *blessed be the name of the Lord!* (Job 1:21)

A second wave of sickness reduces Job to a pitiful caricature of his old self, sitting on ashes and scraping his boils with a potsherd. His wife turns against him and with grim realism she tells him to curse God. Finally, three friends otherwise unknown come to comfort him. They sit silently for seven days. What would they or we say to such a man? What advice will they give Job?

The prologue clearly demands a response from the reader about this extreme case. The readers, too, have experienced unmerited failure, pain and rejection in some way. Will the reader piously agree that Job and the friends should do the right thing by meekly accepting such a fate? Or will they agree with Job's wife? Is some other response possible?

After this spare problem story that was perhaps originally told among some group of rural people, the author adds thirty-six chapters of a violent dispute between Job and the friends who are joined at the end by a young man named Elihu. These friends steadfastly proclaim to Job an extreme view that all his suffering must be due to his sins. Job, true to his description in the

HELP JOB FIND A WAY OUT OF HIS DILEMMA!
God is just [and *must* reward good and punish evil]

God is
All-Powerful

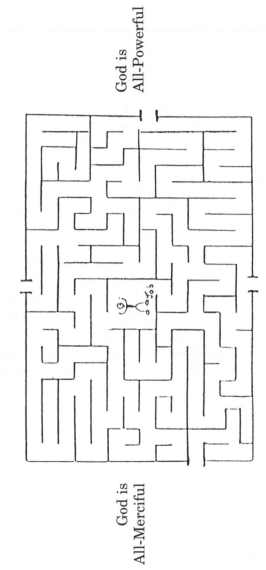

God is free [and can punish good and reward evil]

God is
All-Merciful

prologue, sticks adamantly to his character there and refuses to admit that he has committed any sin, at least one so great as to merit this punishment.

2. The Poetic Dialogue

The text suddenly shifts from a prose narrative to impassioned poetry. Poetry is the language of emotion, not of logic. The images keep tumbling out of the violent dialogue, measured by cadences of balance and antithesis, full of ironies and deliberate confusions. If we are even modestly correct, we are listening to a different language than that of the philosopher or wise man. Is this left-brain or right-brain talk? We are listening to the cry of the people who have suffered in ways similar to Job. And what language will God speak? We will be forced to wait until the end to discover the answer.

But to anticipate the finale, Yahweh will eventually speak to Job. Then the author will add a prose epilogue that is related to the prologue and will bring the story to an end in which God gives it all back and more. It is the happy ending of fairy tales, but not of real life. This poses a final problem because it reverses the entire direction of the dialogues and sheds no light on the book as a realistic story or on our daily problems of unmerited evil.

Clearly the solution of the problem will lie with the readers much more than with the text. From what worldview were the writer or the characters in the dispute coming from? What indications do we have in the text? Is the problem simply upholding the old law of retribution? Proverbs had expressed that view in many of its slices of experience.[3] But had it been made into an immutable principle? Or is the problem one of the acceptance of the mystery of freedom? And, finally, from what worldview or master story do we read this story?[4]

Any good storyteller knows that the middle must explain how the two ends hold together. In this case the middle is a sophisticated dialogue between Job and each of his friends which ends with mutual recriminations. The elaborate cycles of speeches by Job and each of the three friends in turn keep coming back to the same point. The friends hold consistently to their traditional understanding of retribution and even to press it to an extreme conclusion. Although the text does not say that they are Israelites, they obviously belong somewhere in that story. The book was certainly not written for an ecumenical audience. It conjures up the whole tradition of the chosen people until after the Babylonian Captivity. Even then when all of them had suffered a calamity that mirrored Job's and could not paper over their resentment against God, they continued to repeat the old platitudes about retribution down to the third and fourth generation.

The friends at first speak in quiet and conciliatory terms. Their point is that all evil must come from sins that we commit. Job has forgotten the lessons that he himself taught. If only Job will repent, the Lord will reward him with blessings. In this approach they are on the side of Satan, who had suggested that Job was a hypocrite who kept up the appearances of integrity so that the Lord would pay him off with favors.

The Job of the poetry is a different man from the Job of the prologue. His speeches always come with passion. He begins:

> *Perish the day on which I was born,*
> *the night when they said, "The child is a boy!"*

> ...*Why did I not perish at birth,*
> *come forth from the womb and expire?*
> ...*I have no peace nor ease;*
> *I have no rest, for trouble comes!* (Job 3:3, 11, 26)

Later Job ironically takes up the friends' arguments about payment for virtue and scorns them as accusations against God. He uses temper tantrums to confound the benign platitudes of the friends by citing his own justness as described in the prologue. Against that rock-bound coast the waves of the friends smash and retreat. But Job has not been a witness to God's boast and can give no proof that he is truly sinless except on his own word.

From a purely logical analysis, all of this might be stated even more briefly than I have done. But then Job would not be a great book in the estimate of the people who preserved it. Every technique of rhetoric is played in repeated symphonies of order or brilliant dirges. The friends become sarcastic; they claim that Job is no wise man and had never even listened to himself when he had such a reputation. Job accuses the friends of coddling God and distorting the truth to justify him. Job says many of the things that we feel like saying to God in such circumstances but have never had the guts to do so. And he gets nowhere even when he challenges God to write out the indictment against him and bring charges against him.

3. The Wisdom Poem

Then in the middle, when the argument has become white hot, chapter 28 suddenly introduces a poem that seems to undercut all the supposed wisdom these men are bandying back and forth.

> *There is indeed a mine for silver,*
>   *and a place for gold which men refine.*
> *Whence, then, comes wisdom,*
>   *and where is the place of understanding?*
> *The proud beasts have not trodden it,*
>   *nor has the lion gone that way.*
> *The abyss declares, "It is not in me";*
>   *and the sea says, "I have it not."*
> *Abaddon and Death say,*
>   *"Only by rumor have we heard of it."*
> *God knows the way to it;*
>   *it is he who is familiar with its place.*
> *For he beholds the ends of the earth*
>   *and sees all that is under the heavens.*
> *When he made rules for the rain*
>   *and a path for the thunderbolts,*
> *Then he saw wisdom and appraised it,*
>   *gave it its setting, knew it through and through.*
> *And to man he said:*
> *Behold, the fear of the* LORD *is wisdom;*
>   *and avoiding evil is understanding.*
>   (Job 28:1–28 passim)[5]

Order exists in the visible universe, but only God knows what it is. Agur in the Book of Proverbs had despaired of finding the answers because he could not go up to heaven and see it all. Later in the book of Ecclesiastes, Qoheleth will say the same thing. Who knows where wisdom can be found for this case? Only God knows. Apparently all we can do is be in awe of such mysteries.

4. Job's Last Plea

At the end of all the disputations Job's final word is a despairing reassertion of his innocence and a cry for vindication.

> *Oh, that I had one to hear my case,*
>   *and that my accuser would write out his indictment!*
> *Surely, I should wear it on my shoulder*
>   *or put it on me like a diadem;*
> *Of all my steps I should give him an account;*
>   *like a prince I should present myself before him.*
> *This is my final plea; let the Almighty answer me!*
>   *The words of Job are ended.* (Job 31:35–37)

Then a young man named Elihu comes forward to hesitatingly instruct his wise elders.[6] He knows by personal revelation something of a word from God. But one of his words may be the most horrible of all.

> *Look up to the skies and behold;*
>   *regard the heavens high above you.*
> *If you sin, what injury do you do to God?*
>   *Even if your offenses are many, how do you hurt him?*
> *If you are righteous, what do you give him,*
>   *or what does he receive from your hand?*
> *Your wickedness can affect only a man like yourself;*
>   *and your justice only a fellow human being.*
>
> (Job 35:5–8)

Does God care about what you do, either good or bad? Does it even touch him? Or is it all simply a problem among humans, who can hurt only one another? Elihu calls for real repentance. Nobody pays attention to him.

5. The Yahweh Speeches

Finally Yahweh speaks. This is certainly not the language of the ancient story nor that of Job nor that of the friends. If this is God-talk, it sounds like a totally different language. Whoever wrote it understood God-talk. Theologians later defined it as inspired, but the people who accepted it among their sacred books already knew that.

Yahweh might at first seem to be a slightly absent-minded God who ignores the problem and the arguments. He speaks instead of his delight in the order of creation. Why did he make the earth the size that it is? Why do the morning stars sing with joy? Does Job understand why the earth is life-giving? Does he know the secrets of the abyss of the sea, the dwelling place of light and darkness, the storehouse of snow, the thunderstorm, the ice, the stars, the wild animals and their birthing, the free wild ass, the ostrich, the war horse in his strength, the hawk? This speech heaps up all the wonders we can see but do not understand how they came to be.

In the second speech Yahweh asks Job to explain about the mighty creatures who put to shame puny Job. Can he make Behemoth (the hippopotamus) a pet? Can he tame Leviathan (the crocodile)? These are the powerful pagan images of Chaos.

> *Can you play with him, as with a bird?*
> *Can you put him in leash for your maidens?*
> (Job 40:29)

Yahweh delights in what he has made, although Job has spoken as though this is all irrelevant to his one-issue complaint. Yahweh has done all of this out of his free design and his exuberant creativity. He exults in his free

creatures even when, like Job, they irascibly oppose him
in their freedom. Yahweh never despises Job; he respects
him as a man. Twice he addresses Job with respect.

> *Then the* LORD *addressed Job out of the storm and said:*
> *Who is this that obscures divine plans*
>   *with word of ignorance?*
> *Gird up your loins now, like a man;*
>   *I will question you, and you tell me the answers!*
>   (Job 38:1–3 [and 40:6 is similar])

Why all the questions? Clearly they are rhetorical
devices to get honest readers thinking. Jesus in his discourse with Nicodemus asks questions about how much
that teacher in Israel understood where life comes from
or, even more physically, why the wind blows where it
wills.[7] God seems to prefer questions rather than platitudes in speaking to mature people. They must find
their own way with the pointers he gives. Has Job experienced the joy and playfulness of creating all things? Is
his life simply all misery? Does he rejoice in the beautiful and wonderful creatures simply because they are
good? Can Job, a real man, find the answers to these visible things? Job can only hold his tongue.

> *I know that you can do all things,*
>   *and that no purpose of yours can be hindered.*
> *I have dealt with great things that I do not understand;*
>   *things too wonderful for me, which I cannot know.*
> *I had heard of you by word of mouth,*
>   *but now my eye has seen you.*
> *Therefore I disown what I have said,*
>   *and repent in dust and ashes.* (Job 42:2–6)

What did Job repent of?[8] The clearest connection of the
Yahweh speeches with the rest of the book is with the

poem on wisdom in chapter 28. At that point the poem addressed only the problem of Job. Here the quest for wisdom escalates to include all creation in its beauty and playfulness. Job has had a real metacommunication with Yahweh, who shares with him joy instead of sadness.

6. The Epilogue

Job never repented of those hidden sins that his friends had accused him of. Nor was Yahweh looking for that kind of groveling repentance. The epilogue has God saying to Eliphaz:

> *And it came to pass after the LORD had spoken these words to Job, that the LORD said to Eliphaz the Temanite, "I am angry with you and with your two friends; for you have not spoken rightly concerning me, as has my servant Job."* (Job 42:7)

So it was all given back to Job not as payment but as a gift. Job must continue his witnessing to the Lord whom he had seen with his own eyes but whom he had not yet understood.

7. Questioning Retribution

What response should we give to our instinctive retributionist ethic? The only answer possible is one that comes from the metacommunication that the reader supplies by bridging the gap between goodness and evil.

> *"A good person out of the store of goodness in his heart produces good, but an evil person out of a store*

> *of evil produces evil; for from the fullness of the*
> *heart the mouth speaks."* (Luke 6:45)

What was in the heart of the people who wrote and first read this Book of Job? On the one hand, the whole tradition of Israelite religion is involved; on the other, the contentious and inquisitive character of a people. The myths of the good and evil gods, the creation stories of the chosen people, the experience of supposed rejection and companionable respect all contribute to the worldview from which the book was written.

The ancient Israelites had wrestled with the problem of retribution before. At the end they always doubted the extreme view. That long history of the kingdom, which we call the Deuteronomistic history, implacably judged each leader and king on the basis of whether they served the Lord or reached toward idolatry.[9] For example, when the Northern Kingdom was finally destroyed in the eighth century B.C., the prophetic writer wrote a sad commentary on why they deserved what they got (2 Kings 17:7–18).

Jeremiah much later said the same, but more succinctly, of the Southern Kingdom of Judah:

> *Speak to them this word:*
> *Let my eyes stream with tears*
> *   day and night, without rest,*
> *Over the great destruction which overwhelms*
> *   the virgin daughter of my people,*
> *   over her incurable wound.* (Jer 14:17)[10]

And yet the prophets did not seem to accept that the wound was incurable. The true prophet both condemned *and* consoled. The consolation was from the healing God who was not bound by laws of retribution. He did not fully call the people to account for their sins nor did he maintain his anger against them forever.

The final chapters of the Deuteronomic story seem to cast doubts on its own underlying theology of retribution. The Deuteronomist had chronicled five hundred years of the history of Israel and Judah. He had very little good to say about either of them. The last good king was Josiah, a man he praised as a reformer. But Josiah honored a treaty he had made with the Assyrians, and went out with his army to block an invading Egyptian army on the way to Mesopotamia. This reaction has an ironic ending:

> *In his time Pharaoh Neco, king of Egypt, went up toward the river Euphrates to the king of Assyria. King Josiah set out to confront him, but was slain at Megiddo at the first encounter.* (2 Kings 23:29)

And yet nothing at all is said about this tragedy as a retribution, either good or bad. A curtain of silence has descended.[11]

Even more ambiguous on the issue of retribution is the ending of the whole Deuteronomic history. Jerusalem was captured in 597 B.C., its last king, Jehoiachin, led away blinded in disgrace to prison in Babylon. And then we have the climax, the final lesson.

> *In the thirty-seventh year of the exile of Jehoiachin, king of Judah, on the twenty-seventh day of the twelfth month, Evilmerodach, king of Babylon, in the inaugural year of his own reign, raised up Jehoiachin, king of Judah, from prison. He spoke kindly to him and gave him a throne higher than that of the other kings who were with him in Babylon. Jehoiachin took off his prison garb and ate at the king's table as long as he lived. The allowance*

> *granted him by the king was a perpetual allowance,*
> *in fixed daily amounts, for as long as he lived.*
> (2 Kings 25:27–30)

This is a climax? We leave the last king, perpetually eating his meals at a conqueror's table. What was the Deuteronomist waiting for? Is this the common legend of the king who will return? Camelot is drawn from the legend of King Arthur, who waits in Avalon to return as king. The Germans have the story of the Emperor Frederick Barbarossa, who is still sitting at a table in a cave in the Alps, his red beard grown through the stone, while his servant awaits the return of the raven.[12] Hitler loved that. Is this history or a literary perception of reality that lies beyond logic, especially the logic of retribution? Are we forced to look for a metacommunication, as Watzlawick called it, or engage our creative sense of wit in order to understand? Is there a lighthearted view of mystery that calls for play?

8. A Contemporary Mystery

Our contemporary worldview seems to abhor mystery. An answer that ends in mystery is considered unacceptable in academia. Our society at times considers life and death, the beginning and end of the cosmos, the understanding and control of all nature, including us, to be technical problems whose solution lies beyond the next rise in the road. We push forward with amazing success at times. But we are no closer to the final rise than our predecessors.[13] Is there a forbidden frontier? Does the edict against eating from the tree of knowledge really make sense? Would knowing the logic of retribution, good and bad, destroy us? Job was spared at the last. He admitted that he could never know. Was the real problem all along not retribution but acceptance of mystery? Does faith have a hard edge at the limit of mystery?

The retribution theology that Job's friends pushed in its extreme form (which is its usual form) is just too bad to be true. We know that. We are happiest when we have the gifts of love and joy that are unmerited and a God who eventually listens to us. We know salvation most when we reflect on what we have not been punished for.[14] The God of justice is the God of mercy; he is too all-encompassing to be defined by one word or by a theology that insists on keeping the two characteristics separate.

Yet for mercy and justice to kiss, we must take a different tack. The problem of good and evil has always been an irresolvable paradox in our world. The stark juxtaposition of the two images conjures up the basic materials of humor. That is what holds the God of tough love together. It also holds us together. Robert Alter, in *The Art of Biblical Narrative,* remarks on the literary sophistication of the biblical authors. They far exceeded all the ancient pagan writers, because they understood the tension between God's free will and human freedom.[15] Hans Urs von Balthasar has proposed in *Theodramatik* that life is played on a stage without a script.[16] God initiates the dialogue by saying or doing something. Then we must respond in any way we want, with wise or foolish words, virtuous or vicious deeds. But the play goes on as both God and ourselves reveal our characters in this drama. But we can't stay around on this planet for the ending. Only wit can project.

George Bernard Shaw tried desperately to denounce Christianity as harsh. He said of Paul: "It was Paul who converted the religion that has raised one man above sin and death into a religion that delivered millions of men so completely into their dominion that their own common nature became a horror to them, and the religious life became a denial of life." G. K. Chesterton, his great opponent in those arguments, remarked that Shaw "does not allow for that deeper sort of paradox by which two opposite cords of truth become entangled in an inextricable knot. Still less can he be made to realize that it is often this knowledge which ties safely together the whole bundle of human life." The humor of paradox keeps us Christian.

No one has ever explained the whole Book of Job in a convincing way. The litany of those who have tried runs from the ancients to modern dramatists and photographers and scholars.[17] Yet Job remains one of the most popular books of the Bible and is hailed as a literary masterpiece. Is it odd that this one great book has no clear answer? Whatever answer the reader gives will not come from logic but from experience and imagination—either metacommunication or the grace of God.

6

Qoheleth, the Gentle Critic

1. The Tedium of Change

The Book of Ecclesiastes, or Qoheleth as it is called in Hebrew, will serve as an example of what I am inclined to call a survivor's handbook. The book begins with a well-known poem:

Vanity of vanities, says Qoheleth,
vanity of vanities! All things are vanity!
What profit has man from all the labor
which he toils at under the sun?
One generation passes and another comes,
but the world forever stays.
The sun rises and the sun goes down;
then it presses on to the place where it rises.
Blowing now toward the south, then toward the north,
the wind turns again and again, resuming its rounds.
All rivers go to the sea,
yet never does the sea become full.
To the place where they go,
the rivers keep on going.
All speech is labored;
there is nothing man can say.
The eye is not satisfied with seeing
nor is the ear filled with hearing. (Eccl 1:2–8)

"Cast your bread upon water"
Ecclesiastes 11:1

The heaping up of such parallel images is a common technique of rhetoric. The effect is to give a picture of order that goes nowhere. We have our own shorter modern saying: "The more things change, the more they stay the same." Both Qoheleth's and ours are observations of the common people, but Qoheleth's is better because it is poetic and conjures up more images. Luis Alonso Schökel made a helpful distinction between scientific language (which conveys no feelings), poetic language (which depends on feelings and moods and images) and popular language which is closer to the poetic than to the scientific).[1] Qoheleth has created the poetic mood at the beginning to define the problem he wishes to address.

2. The Frustration of Order

Job began with an imaginary story about a perfect character. Qoheleth did something of the same by casting himself as Solomon. Unlike Job who had it all taken away, Qoheleth got to keep it all. He was condemned to live with wealth, power, enjoyment, good wine, servants, female singers and wisdom. Eventually he found them all tedious (Eccl 1:12—2:17). Like Job he loathed life.

The good things of life were as transitory as a breath—vanity. Or was it absurdity?[2] The Hebrew word *hebel* could mean either. Wealth and power passed to a foolish heir too often, pleasure was for the moment, and wisdom itself provoked grief:

> *For in much wisdom there is much sorrow,*
> *and he who stores up knowledge stores up grief.*
> (Eccl 1:18)

Was it absurd to work so hard for peace and joy and justice when the experience of so many of us was that it escaped us in the end and the old evils returned? And what was the irony? Did we instinctively measure life by our own hidden agendas and find them overturned in the end? The wise man indeed had an advantage.

> *The wise man has eyes in his head,*
> *but the fool walks in darkness.*
> *Yet I knew that one lot befalls both of them.* (Eccl 2:14)

Who was the fool? Irony can be either bitter and damning or playful and gentle. And if it was ironic but not despairing, could we absorb it without a touch of wit?

The wise always sought to find order in the recurring events of life. This wise man discovered merely repetition.

> *There is an appointed time for everything,*
>   *and a time for every affair under the heavens.*
> *A time to be born, and a time to die;*
>   *a time to plant, and a time to uproot the plant.*
> *A time to kill, and a time to heal;*
>   *a time to tear down, and a time to build.*
> *A time to weep, and a time to laugh;*
>   *a time to mourn, and a time to dance.*
> *A time to scatter stones, and a time to gather them;*
>   *a time to embrace, and a time to be far from embraces.*
> *A time to seek, and a time to lose;*
>   *a time to keep, and a time to cast away.*
> *A time to rend, and a time to sew;*
>   *a time to be silent, and a time to speak.*
> *A time to love, and a time to hate;*
>   *a time of war, and a time of peace.* (Eccl 3:1–8)

The Vietnam era turned it into a protest song against war, but we didn't protest enough about life in general.

Why these things keep coming back despite our goodness or our badness seems to be the problem. What we want is the timeless.

> *What advantage has the worker from his toil? I have considered the task which God has appointed for men to be busied about. He has made everything appropriate to its time, and has put the timeless into their hearts, without men's ever discovering, from beginning to end, the work which God has done. I recognized that there is nothing better than to be glad and to do well during life. For every man, moreover, to eat and drink and enjoy the fruit of all his labor is a gift of God...Thus has God done that he may be revered. What now is has already been; what is to be, already is; and God restores what would otherwise be displaced.* (Eccl 3:9–15)[3]

"And God restores what would otherwise be displaced."
Where did that come from except from a long faith experience?

3. Qoheleth as a Teacher

*Besides being wise, Qoheleth taught the people
knowledge, and weighed, scrutinized and arranged
many proverbs. Qoheleth sought to find pleasing
sayings and to write down these sayings with precision.* (Eccl 12:9–10)[4]

As a wise teacher, Qoheleth knew that getting students
to ask good questions was more important than feeding
them comforting conclusions. The editor of the book
wrote at the end:

*The sayings of the wise are like goads; like fixed
spikes are the topics given by one collector.*
(Eccl 12:11)

Proverbs often goad us into thought by accentuating contraries, but spikes are needed to hang them all together
on our walls. The clothes hanging on pegs in an entranceway do a lot to define the character of the occupant.

Qoheleth goaded readers largely by satire. Satire,
like irony; can be bitter in exposing our folly, or it can be
gentle in persuading us to look beyond. Qoheleth lampooned himself in a satirical little parable.

*On the other hand I saw this wise deed under the
sun, which I thought sublime. Against a small city
with few men in it advanced a mighty king, who surrounded it and threw up great siegeworks about it.
But in the city lived a man who, though poor, was*

> *wise, and he delivered it through his wisdom. Yet no*
> *one remembered this poor man. Though I had said,*
> *"Wisdom is better than force," yet the wisdom of the*
> *poor man is despised and his words go unheeded.*
>
> (Eccl 9:13–16)

Is there something beyond even successful wisdom? Can one find anything that is real and lasting? That is the question which Qoheleth set himself to address. We expect success from hard work. Does experience confirm that it is so? Or must we look for something different or beyond?

The touch of wit in proverbs has already been noted. Qoheleth destroys too many platitudes to be taken without the proverbial grain of salt, or to vary the image, without the proverbial tongue in cheek. In the middle of the book Qoheleth turns some of the ancient proverbs head over heels.

> *A good name is better than good ointment,*
>   *and the day of death than the day of birth.*
> *It is better to go to the house of mourning*
>   *than to the house of feasting....*
> *Sorrow is better than laughter,*
>   *because when the face is sad the heart grows wiser.*
> *The heart of the wise is in the house of mourning,*
>   *but the heart of fools is in the house of mirth.*
>
> (Eccl 7:1–4)

Of course, he also says five times that one should eat, drink and be merry, which certainly sounds strange here.[5]

> *Go, eat your bread with joy and drink your wine*
> *with a merry heart, because it is now that God*
> *favors your works. At all times let your garments be*

*white, and spare not the perfume for your head.
Enjoy life with the wife whom you love, all the days
of the fleeting life that is granted you under the sun.
This is your lot in life, for the toil of your labors
under the sun. Anything you can turn your hand to,
do with what power you have; for there will be no
work, nor reason, nor knowledge, nor wisdom in the
nether world where you are going.* (Eccl 9:7–10)

Yet it is a serious problem he is discussing, not just good
living.

4. Qoheleth as Social Critic

Some commentators accuse Qoheleth of being a
Stoic, a man who withdrew from the strife of public life
to find comfort within himself. He certainly was not a
radical attacking the social system or a prophet fore-
telling doom or an activist. He seemed content to position himself as a spectator, but it was not for the usual
reasons. Perhaps he was taking a different approach in
those days after the Babylonian Captivity when fidelity
to Yahweh seemed to produce no justice.

The popular notion of retribution seems to be that
good is always rewarded with benefits and evil with punishment. That was the extreme position taken by the
friends of Job. The problem then as now was that it does
not always work. Qoheleth noted that order seemed to be
mere repetition. The sun, the rivers, the desire to see
and know all pursued an endless course and never got
anywhere. There was a time for everything—birth and
death, war and peace, love and hate. Our good and evil
doing seemed to have no effect on it. Qoheleth looks at
the Temple and says:

> *Meanwhile I saw wicked men approach and enter;*
> *and as they left the sacred place, they were praised*
> *in the city for what they had done. This also is van-*
> *ity. Because the sentence against evildoers is not*
> *promptly executed, therefore the hearts of men are*
> *filled with the desire to commit evil—because the*
> *sinner does evil a hundred times and survives.*
> *Though indeed I know that it shall be well with*
> *those who fear God, for their reverence toward him;*
> *and that it shall not be well with the wicked man,*
> *and he shall not prolong his shadowy days, for his*
> *lack of reverence toward God. This is a vanity*
> *which occurs on earth: there are just men treated as*
> *though they had done evil and wicked men treated*
> *as though they had done justly. This, too, I say is*
> *vanity.* (Eccl 8:10–14)

This law of retribution seemed to have run in reverse.
Qoheleth looks at the government and writes:

> *If you see oppression of the poor, and violation of*
> *rights and justice in the realm, do not be shocked by*
> *the fact, for the high official has another higher than*
> *he watching him and above these are others higher*
> *still—. Yet an advantage for a country in every*
> *respect is a king for the arable land.* (Eccl 5:7–8)

We sometimes say the same thing about government. We
don't like the corruption, but it is better than having no
government at all.

5. Qoheleth's Advice

So what advice did Qoheleth finally give? He
remembered his youth with its joyful enthusiasms and
its high ideals. He had lived to attain much of them and

found achievement hollow. He had to look to the future in which God still would not reveal all his plans but would be there. He had the faith that the whole tradition of Judaism had fostered in him. It is against that background of his mature view of life that he gives his final instruction.

The end of the book discloses the mystery in its fullness. The old teacher had told his young pupils:

> *Rejoice, O young man, while you are young*
> *and let your heart be glad in the days of your youth.*
> *Follow the ways of your heart,*
> *The vision of your eyes;*
> *Yet understand that as regards all this*
> *God will bring you to judgment.* (Eccl 11:9–10)

The judgment is not "final judgment" as we usually think, but that judgment which life reveals. For himself in old age, however, Qoheleth paints a hauntingly beautiful picture of his last wistful walk through the deserted village of his life.

> *Remember your Creator in the days of your youth,*
> *before the evil days come*
> *And the years approach of which you will say,*
> *I have no pleasure in them;*
> *Before the sun is darkened*
> *and the light, and the moon, and the stars,*
> *while the clouds return after the rain;*
> *When one waits for the chirp of a bird,*
> *but all the daughters of song are suppressed;*
> *And one fears heights,*
> *and perils in the street;*
> *Because man goes to his lasting home,*
> *and mourners go about the streets;*
> *Before the silver cord is snapped*
> *and the golden bowl is broken,*

> *And the pitcher is shattered at the spring,*
> *and the broken pulley falls into the well,*
> *And the dust returns to the earth as it once was,*
> *and the life breath returns to God who gave it.*
> *Vanity of vanities, says Qoheleth,*
> *all things are vanity!* (Eccl 12:1–8 passim)

"[T]he life breath returns to God who gave it"![6] Qoheleth does not say how. But he does say it very beautifully and it appeals especially to those who are old. It is the overriding conviction of his faith that returns him to the presence of God. This is the "fixed spike" on which it all hangs. So he can dare to say, as most of the wisdom writers did, that "The fear of the Lord is the beginning of wisdom."[7] Our very limited experiences of life, often divergent, can be bundled together only by tying it all together with faith and a poetic paradox. In the end, that is the literary entry into mystery.[8]

6. What Shall We Say of Qoheleth?

Perhaps Robert Gordis has best caught the tone of the book. Gordis, a rabbi, pictures Qoheleth as the teacher at a celebration when his old students had come to visit him.[9] Some are now important government officials, others are Temple dignitaries, others have far-flung economic interests as merchant princes or landed gentry. Qoheleth remembers the shining, carefree countenances of youth, the sparkling eyes brimful with mischief. Those are gone. In their stead are worn faces, some drawn, others grown puffy with the years, and tired, unhappy eyes sagging beneath the weight of responsibility. He notes that they have paid a high price for success. He knows what they have forgotten—that people's schemes and projects, their petty jealousies and labors, their struggles and heartaches are all vanity and that joy in life is the one divine commandment. So he wrote his book to remind them and himself of what was not vanity. And so a masterpiece was born.

What is the problem of Qoheleth? The problem, as with Job, is that *we expect* God to render to each of us according to our deeds and as we make the rules.[10] We call it a law of retribution. We learn as children that doing wrong leads to punishment. We see hard work being rewarded by a pay increase and we expect it. With all their observation of the way men act, the sages noted this and admired an order in the universe. The discipline of order and achievement with its rewards and punishments seemed perfectly satisfactory to them and made for a peaceful life. We continue to wish for the same today. But there is no way to fix all the inequities and injustices.

Job had to suffer unjustified calamity. Qoheleth had to suffer unmerited success, and he found it vanity; his golden coin was a mere Mardi Gras doubloon, not honest gold. It wasn't worth all the ceaseless work. Is that all there is? In the end, the problem remained: Was there retribution, or instead, mystery?

7. The Voice of the People and Qoheleth

So how did this book come to be accepted as a word of God? This is a book of wisdom, but not the total wisdom. Agur had despaired of going up to the heavens to be able to see all that was happening in the world and so acquire wisdom itself. The poem in Job had despaired of finding where wisdom is hidden in the world. Yet these men continued to be good Jews. Qoheleth could comfortably accept his life as a chase after the wind. He knew that God was still watching the chase.

The Jewish people were unique in believing in and worshiping one God. That one God was above all gods because he was wholly what God should be—righteous yet gentle, intimate as well as remote. He was not just all mighty; he was also close to them as no other god is close to his people.[11] He was everywhere, but he had a place in the Temple. He gave life and he gave death; sometimes he seemed ruthless in destroying and at other times as tender as a bridegroom at the wedding banquet. He was all this and much more. No one could tie together logically all the different strands in God. And no one could say the one word that expressed it all. The common people appreciated Qoheleth.[12]

He spoke their language and dared to express the human feelings of his people and of us about injustice and vanity among a conventional people who dared not say it. His words are the words of a poet who captured by sound and image what scientific language could never do. This old man, full of doubts, could write that hauntingly evocative poem at the end. "The life breath returns to God who gave it."

That is what the people believed. So they embraced this curious book within their canon of sacred books which proclaimed what they saw themselves to be—embattled survivors in the game of life. Qoheleth knew that all is in the hands of God. Joy and peace are gifts not rewards, and punishment is to be meted out cautiously.

7

The Comic Story of Jonah

1. Jonah and the Friendly Fish

Beyond doubt, Jonah is the funniest book in the Bible. Some unknown writer after the Babylonian Exile wanted to comment on a false popular belief that the enemies of the Jews were about to be eliminated.[1] The Lord had promised prosperity to Israel and almost as often through the prophets destruction of their enemies. After the Babylonian Exile some Jews wanted the Lord to deliver destruction now. That, they thought, was the value of prophets. But were these true prophets or false ones?[2]

The author chose a wonderfully whimsical form to tell a story of what might happen if such a successful prophet of this sort really appeared. He cribbed the name of his antihero from the only prophet in their tradition who had foretold success and lived to see it happen. The traditional record of the reign of Jeroboam II (786 to 746 B.C.) read:

> *He restored the boundaries of Israel from Labo-of-*
> *Hamath to the sea of the Arabah, just as the LORD,*
> *the God of Israel, had prophesied through his*

servant, the prophet Jonah, son of Amittai, from Gath-hepher. (2 Kgs 14:25)

The prophetic author of Kings introduced his account of Jeroboam: "He did evil in the sight of the LORD; he did not desist from any of the sins which Jeroboam, son of Nebat, had caused Israel to commit" (2 Kgs 14:24). Then comes the saying about Jonah. This Jonah knew the real reason why Jeroboam was a success. "Since the LORD had not determined to blot out the name of Israel from under the heavens, he saved them through Jeroboam, son of Joash" (2 Kgs 14:26).

The prophecy, however, had been misunderstood to predict permanent prosperity. Twenty-five years later the Lord determined to blot out the name of Israel, and in 721 B.C. the kingdom of Israel was destroyed forever. The king had been doomed by success in manipulating religion to serve his own political policies.

The people, however, had never taken the admonitions of the prophets very seriously. Two hundred years or more later, they still wanted prophets of prosperity, not the stern reprimands of true prophets. Our author conjectured: What would happen if the Lord sent a prophet of conversion who succeeded? Who would be converted? This is the comic premise of the story. At the end Nineveh is not destroyed and Jonah is rebuked. The incongruous, the contradictory, is the essence of comedy, as both Hazlitt and Kierkegaard have noted.

First, the story opens with a chuckle. The word of the Lord came to this fictional Jonah of Amittai to preach in Nineveh. Preaching about the one true God to the pagans who had destroyed Jerusalem was totally ludicrous. Jonah went down to Joppa and booked passage on the first boat he could find heading in the opposite direction to Tarshish. The Lord stopped that quickly.

He sent a great storm that terrified the sailors. When the ship was in danger of breaking up, they cried, each one to his god. As everyone knew, disaster meant that the gods were angry. However, the sea itself was the symbol of chaos where no order exists. Their local gods did not have much power. Next they jettisoned the cargo to lighten the ship. That didn't work. When the sailors began pointing fingers at one another, the captain finally went below and woke up Jonah. Jonah, the landlubber, had slept through it all. The captain demanded that Jonah call on his God as the rest had done. "Perhaps God will be mindful of us so that we may not perish" (Jonah 1:6).

Jonah admitted that he was the guilty party; on the trip out he had told the sailors that he was fleeing from the Lord who ruled both the sea and the land. He knew what was happening. So he told the crew to throw him overboard.

When they did, the Lord sent a large friendly fish to swallow up Jonah gently. Sea monsters were usually symbols of chaos, but this one was operating on the Lord's plan. In this animated submarine Jonah composed a psalm. Well, really he didn't make it all up. It is suspiciously like most other laments in the psalms. But it has delightful touches about Jonah's experiences in the belly of the fish.

> *The waters swirled about me, threatening my life;*
> *the abyss enveloped me;*
> *seaweed clung about my head.*
> *Down I went to the roots of the mountains;*
> *the bars of the nether world*
> *were closing behind me forever,*
> *But you brought my life up from the pit,*
> *O LORD, my God.* (Jonah 2:6–7)

That was enough psalmmaking for the Lord; he commanded the fish to spew Jonah up on the shore.

2. The Nineveh Scene

Then the story begins again with the Lord's instruction to set out for Nineveh. Jonah headed for Nineveh across the desert. He walked through the imposing gates of that metropolis to the first square and announced: "Forty days and Nineveh will be destroyed!" Everything stopped. The pagans believed and proclaimed a great fast and all of them put on sackcloth.

When word of this reached the king on his throne, he laid aside his robe, fasted and sat on ashes. Then he issued a royal decree that not only every person in his realm but all the beasts, cattle and sheep, should do likewise. And so we are left with the prophet in the midst of all those repentant sinners. Even the cattle were standing before their troughs, covered with sackcloth and ashes, not daring to take a bite or lap the water. Nothing like this had ever happened among the chosen people.

And the prophet of doom? When God himself had repented, Jonah was left in the lurch. He was angry.

> *"I beseech you, LORD," he prayed, "is not this what I said while I was still in my own country? This is why I fled at first to Tarshish. I knew that you are a gracious and merciful God, slow to anger, rich in clemency, loathe to punish. And now, LORD, please take my life from me; for it is better for me to die than to live."* (Jonah 4:2–3)

But it wasn't so easy. Jonah needed to deal with the Lord who doesn't provide easy escapes.

But the LORD asked, "Have you reason to be angry?"
(Jonah 4:4)

So Jonah went off pouting. A deal is a deal and Jonah was going to hold the Lord accountable. He went outside the city and built a shelter where he could watch the inevitable destruction of Nineveh in comfort. When the sun came up, the Lord caused a gourd plant to grow over Jonah; it was as comfortable as being in the belly of the fish. But the next morning at dawn God sent a worm that caused the plant to wither. Jonah had a low tolerance for this kind of treatment and asked again for death.

> *But God said to Jonah, "Have you reason to be angry over the plant?" "I have reason to be angry," Jonah answered, "angry enough to die." Then the LORD said, "You are concerned over the plant which cost you no labor and which you did not raise; it came up in one night and in one night it perished. And should I not be concerned over Nineveh, the great city, in which there are more than a hundred and twenty thousand persons who cannot distinguish their right hand from their left, not to mention the many cattle?"* (Jonah 4:9–11)

"Not to mention the many cattle?" A master stroke of artistry.

What reaction would those readers in Jerusalem, still smarting over the cruelty of Nineveh, have had? What reaction do we have in reading this book? We can understand the Jewish hatred of Nineveh. Even later Daniel lamented:

> *We have in our day no prince, prophet, or leader, no holocaust, sacrifice, oblation, or incense, no place to offer first fruits, to find favor with you.* (Dan 3:38)

Nineveh had been responsible for it all, and were the pagans now to escape scot-free? Where was the fidelity of the Lord to all those curses the prophets had hurled against their enemies? Was the prophet to be made a fool of? Why be a chosen people only to be given second place? Could the people of postexilic Judaism see Jonah in themselves as they grumbled about others being saved? Was this all that prophecy amounted to in the end? Broken promises? So God inspired a man to write this whimsical tale. And God laughed. Like Job's God, he delighted in his creation, all of it.

3. The Humor of the Jonah Story

Such lighthearted pictures can be found rather extensively in the Bible, but they must be pictured. Proverbs endlessly poke fun at human follies. "Though you should pound the fool to bits with pestle, amid the grits in a mortar, his folly will not go out of him" (Prov 27:32). "The door turns on its hinges, the sluggard, on his bed" (Prov 26:14). "A man who has a bribe to offer rates it a magic stone, at every turn it brings him success" (Prov 17:8). The historical background I have given helps somewhat to see the story, but we understand it quickly even without that.

One enjoys the humor of Jonah without bothering much about the technical details of how the master storyteller did it. We grasp immediately the opposing characterizations of the cranky, self-centered Jonah and the God who takes joy in all his creation. That is enough to trigger our laughter. Yet sophisticated artistry is behind the effect produced, and the details that we do not explicitly notice lead us to deeper meaning.[3] Humor, as noted previously, depends on strong contrasts. This story proceeds regularly by binary structures. Only two principal characters are in the plot: the Lord and Jonah. The story is balanced between two sections: the fish section in chapters 1 and 2, and the Nineveh section in chapters 3 and 4. Each begins with the "word of the Lord" in 1:1 and 3:1. The sailors invoke their gods in 1:14–16 and the Ninevites believed God in 3:5 and cried loudly to him in 3:8. The Lord rescued Jonah by the fish in the first story; he rescued him again from the heat by the gourd plant in the second. Jonah complains twice that he might as well die. In 4:3 he begs God to take his life, "for it is better for me to die than to live"; in 4:8 he again begs: "I would be better off dead than alive." God has two answers. His first is in true Jewish fashion by another question: "Have you reason to be angry?" (4:4); in the second God is more specific: "Have you reason to be angry over the plant?" (4:9). One absorbs these binary contrasts without effort and finds them amusing.

However, the story becomes richer the more we pay attention. Jonah and God are characterized as quite opposite. The first word of the Lord is generic: "Set out for the great city of Nineveh and preach against it; their wickedness has come up before me" (Jonah 1:1). Jonah agrees with only the wickedness part. Nothing is said about "forty days and Nineveh will be destroyed." In the second word the Lord tells Jonah simply to set out for Nineveh and "announce the message that I will tell you" (Jonah 3:1). Apparently, Jonah makes up the "forty days and Nineveh will be destroyed" (Jonah 3:4). That was approximately the only part that he had accepted to begin with. It also seems to be what his audience expects. When God repented, Jonah suspected that he wasn't going to get what he wanted, and so he peevishly complained: "Is this not what I said while I was still in my own country? That is why I fled at first to Tarshish.

I knew that you are a gracious and merciful God, slow to anger, rich in clemency, loathe to punish" (Jonah 4:2). So he blames God for his anger.

God does not say or do much until his final speech. He had shown himself the master of the storm and the fish in the first half of the story. He has used few words in the Nineveh scene, and growing a gourd plant is not all that impressive for "the Lord, the God of heaven, who made the sea and the dry land" (Jonah 1:9). So we are surprised by how voluble he is in his last speech. And how delightfully wise he is.

4. The Prophetic Message and Humor

A similar mingling of prophecy and wisdom is found with high humor in the story of Balaam (Num 22:2—24:25). Balaam was a pagan soothsayer who was paid by the king of Edom to curse Israel. All his traditional rituals could not control God, who is free. God contradicted Balaam through a talking ass and an invisible angel. At the end, Balaam pronounced the blessing on Israel, which was the doom of Edom.

Whether one describes the Book of Jonah as prophecy or wisdom, this people's story ends with the good God of creation. Jonah himself had been saved from his disobedience by the fish. Was he ever saved from his own bitterness? Could the audience who heard this master story see themselves in it? Were they, the Chosen People who had finally embraced monotheism in the Captivity, now going to await the destruction of all the idolaters whom they had so recently left? Had they become prophets of doom for all other people? Not to mention the cattle?

Without the whole story of the Bible, Jonah is simply a clever tale. In the beginning, as the people knew, God made all things and pronounced them good. The creatures most like himself, his own people, had deliberately rejected his goodness all during their history. Yet through the ages some of them continued to praise the fidelity and goodness of God. Jonah himself did so in his psalm even while he was fleeing from the Lord. Salvation and a return to primal goodness was always possible. The goodness of the Creator is a common theme in both prophecy and wisdom.

We sometimes complain that the Old Testament is primitive literature that has little to say to our world of sophisticated communications. In truth, as Robert Alter views the situation, we are the primitives in reading many biblical stories and miss the sophistication. We understand something, but not all. And we deprive ourselves of the opportunity of rising to the level of God. Only a touch of humor can lift us up.

8

Wisdom in Late Judaism

1. The Later Quest for Wisdom

The pursuit of Lady Wisdom seems to have faltered for several centuries in postexilic Judaism. However, as new threats to Jewish pragmatic wisdom emerged, two new reinterpretations from different worldviews emerged. First, Ben Sirach, a conservative teacher in Jerusalem, wrote a book between 200 and 175 B.C. that continued the old proverbial approach. The concrete forms of wisdom for him were the scrolls of the Law, which he could hold in his hands. With the Law went all those signs of God's presence that could be clearly seen—the Temple, the priests, the cult.

The persecution of the Jews by the Hellenistic Seleucid emperors who controlled Palestine was just a few years ahead. The time would come shortly when possessing the scrolls could bring death. Sirach was preparing his faithful students to survive the Greek attempt to remold Jews into good pagans. Ironically, the text has come down to us mostly in its Alexandrian Greek version!

On the other hand, the Book of the Wisdom of Solomon was composed by a Jewish teacher in Alexandria about 100 B.C. His immediate image of wisdom was the lifestyle of the Jewish ghetto, which was both inclusive and exclusive in many ways. Although these Jews had melded somewhat into the Hellenistic culture of Alexandria, they were still distinct by dress, language and most of all by synagogue worship. While the pagans attended gymnasia as their meeting places, the Jews gathered in their synagogues. The city had its splendid temples and statues to the gods. Learning and wisdom were held in high esteem, as evidenced by its world-famous library. These Egyptians had adopted with enthusiasm the whole Greek way of life. They despised the Jews. Sometimes it went beyond racial slurs; riots erupted and Jews were killed.

The Jews built up their own library in Greek, especially the translations of the sacred books of Israel. All these stories and prophetic teachings and wisdom writings embodied a far nobler view of life than pagans espoused. Judaism was far superior to the mystic mythologies of Egypt or the imported philosophies of Greece. To preserve his people from the alluring attractions of this pagan culture with its brilliant art and poetry and its proclamation of freedom, this Jewish teacher juxtaposed the wisdom of their traditions. For the Jews, wisdom was more than a goddess, more than an intellectual exercise. It was, indeed, the very spirit of God himself.

2. The Wisdom of Ben Sirach

Sirach begins with a poem to wisdom much as Proverbs did (Sir 1:1–18). It too centers on the fear of the Lord as the beginning of wisdom (Sir 1:9,10,11,12,14, 16,18). Yet Sirach still knows the joy and timelessness of wisdom.

> *All wisdom comes from the LORD*
> *and with him it remains forever.*
> *The sand of the seashore, the drops of rain,*
> *the days of eternity: who can number these?*
> *Heaven's height, earth's breadth,*
> *the depths of the abyss: who can explore these?*
> *Before all things else wisdom was created;*
> *and prudent understanding, from eternity.* (Sir 1:1–4)

Most of the book is taken up with miscellaneous proverbs (Sir 1:19—42:14), sometimes arranged almost in essay style as the author groups similar proverbs. Ben Sirach's proverbs tend to be more ponderous and platitudinous than the earlier ones.

> *Of sharing the expenses of a business or a journey,*
> *or of dividing an inheritance or property;*
> *Of accuracy of scales and balances,*
> *or of tested measures and weights....* (Sir 42:3–4)

Robert Alter called Proverbs "the poetry of wit"; one would need to stretch the observation to say the same of Sirach.[1] Still, Jewish readers knew how to respond to this rhetoric, so much tied were they to practical affairs.

Distinctive of Ben Sirach in late Judaism is his emphasis on the Law as setting the right Way. When this wisdom reaches for the sky, they can understand it:

> *Before all ages, in the beginning, he created me,*
> *and through all ages I shall not cease to be.*
> *Come to me, all you that yearn for me,*
> *and be filled with my fruits;*
> *You will remember me as sweeter than honey,*
> *better to have than the honeycomb.*
> *He who eats of me will hunger still,*
> *he who drinks of me will thirst for more;*
> *...All this is true of the book of the Most High's*

covenant, the law which Moses commanded us
as an inheritance for the community of Jacob.
(Sir 24:9, 18–20, 22)

The little girl of creation is still shyly in the background.

At the end of the proverbs Ben Sirach writes a delightful poem in praise of God in nature. It begins:

Now will I recall God's works;
what I have seen, I will describe.
At God's word were his works brought into being;
they do his will as he has ordained for them.
(Sir 42:15)

Then it goes on:

Let us praise him the more, since we cannot fathom him,
for greater is he than all his works;
Awful indeed is the LORD's majesty,
and wonderful is his power.
For who can see him and describe him?
or who can praise him as he is?
Beyond these, many things lie hid;
only a few of his works have we seen.
(Sir 43:29–30, 33–34)

We will meet this creative Word of God again in the Prologue of John's Gospel.

The final section of Sirach is entitled "Praise of Israel's Ancestors." This long catalog is not a list of proverbs but rather an essay on a curious selection of heroes that has always defied our modern analysis.[2] Yet it was esteemed and deemed relevant to traditionalist Jews of the time. The Epistle to the Hebrews has a somewhat similar listing in chapter 11. Abel, Noah, Abraham, Moses, Rahab (the harlot of Jericho), Jephthah (the chieftain who

"Take a potter"
Wisdom 15:7

sacrificed his daughter to God in thanks for overcoming his enemies), the woman of Maccabean times who saw all of her seven sons martyred for their loyalty to Yahweh, prophets and the fugitives in times of persecution all enter into this curious list. But the theme here is clear: "Faith is the realization of what is hoped for and evidence of things not seen. Because of it the ancients were well attested" (Heb 11:1–2). Sirach would have understood that paradox. That is the way of wisdom.

Sirach delights in the paradoxes, the opposites and the reversals that he sees in the teeming life around him. So too did the common people as they shrewdly assigned a place to their own friends and neighbors within God's designs:

So too, all men are of clay,
    for from earth man was formed;

> *Yet with his great knowledge the LORD makes men unlike;*
> *in different paths he has them walk.*
> *Some he blesses and makes great,*
> *some he sanctifies and draws to himself.*
> *Others he curses and brings low,*
> *and expels them from their place.*
> *Like clay in the hands of a potter,*
> *to be molded according to his pleasure,*
> *So are men in the hands of their Creator,*
> *to be assigned by him their function.*
> *As evil contrasts with good, and death with life,*
> *so are sinners in contrast with the just;*
> *See now all the works of the Most High:*
> *they come in pairs, the one the opposite of the other.*
>
> (Sir 33:10–15)

The people knew that. "See now all the works of the Most High: they come in pairs, the one the opposite of the other." The true God must always stand in tension against the other gods, the good against the evil. That is the mystery and the paradox that begets unity.

3. The Wisdom of Solomon

The author of the Wisdom of Solomon is more attuned to wit in the sense of paradox and playful irony than was Sirach. Walking around Alexandria, overawed by the impressive but oppressive power of the government and its public religion, he turned to his Jewish God. Jews of the ghetto were being led astray; some of them had died in riots or persecutions. The brilliant Greek culture, whose key words were *freedom* and *beauty,* was false-faced. His own satire was cutting as he pictured what the pleasure-loving Greeks were saying:

> *For our lifetime is the passing of a shadow;*
>   *and our dying cannot be deferred*
>   *because it is fixed with a seal; and no one returns.*
> *Come, therefore, let us enjoy the good things that are real,*
>   *and use the freshness of creation avidly.*
> *Let us have our fill of costly wine and perfumes,*
>   *and let no springtime blossom pass us by;*
>   *let us crown ourselves with rosebuds ere they wither.*
> *Let no meadow be free from our wantonness;*
>   *everywhere let us leave tokens of our rejoicing,*
>   *for this our portion is, and this our lot.* (Wis 2:5–9)

A dark side inhabits freedom for the oppressed:

> *Let us oppress the needy just man;*
>   *let us neither spare the widow*
>   *nor revere the old man for his hair grown white with time.*
> *But let our strength be our norm of justice;*
>   *for weakness proves itself useless.* (Wis 2:10–11)

The veneer of Greek freedom bolstered by philosophy had no solid wood behind it. In this chapter we can only take a small walk ourselves around the Book of the Wisdom of Solomon. For example, in all the government offices of Egypt the mandatory image of the Pharaoh was hung. This is how Wisdom explains its origins:

> *For a father, afflicted with untimely mourning,*
>   *made an image of the child so quickly taken from him,*
> *And now honored as a god what was formerly a dead man*
>   *and handed down to his subjects mysteries and*
>   *sacrifices.*
> *Then, in time, the impious practice gained strength and*
>   *was observed as law,*
>   *and graven things were worshiped by princely decrees.*
> *Men who lived so far away that they could not honor him*
>   *in his presence*

copied the appearance of the distant king
And made a public image of him they wished to honor,
out of zeal to flatter him when absent, as though present.
And to promote this observance among those to whom it
was strange,
the artisan's ambition provided a stimulus.

(Wis 14:15–18)

Thus this wise Jewish teacher in the Greek world reinvigorated for his people, caught in an alien culture, the older prophetic technique of "spoofing the gods," which had begun with Jeremiah in the original Semitic world.[3]

It is within such a context of addictive idolatry that the nobler thoughts of Wisdom take shape as paradox. One cannot kill the Jew; he lives forever.

"…Let us condemn him to a shameful death;
for according to his own words, God will take care of
him."
These were their thoughts, but they erred;
for their wickedness blinded them,
For God formed man to be imperishable;
the image of his own nature he made him.

(Wis 2:20–21,23)

In contrast to the live-for-today pleasure seeking of the Greeks stood the immortality of the Jew. One could see the contrast right in Egypt. The ancient Egyptian dynasties had passed away although the pyramids and the temples remained. The great library of Alexandria and the temples of Isis and other mystery gods and goddesses now ruled the city. The government was that of foreigners, of whom Cleopatra was the most famous. This oppressive power of the culture and the government too would pass. Faithful Jews and their God, however, would remain ever alive:

For your might is the source of justice;
  your mastery over all things makes you lenient to all.
For you show your might when the perfection of your
  power is disbelieved;
  and in those who know you,
  you rebuke temerity.
But though you are master of might, you judge
  with clemency, and with much lenience you govern us;
  for power, whenever you will, attends you.

(Wis 12:16–18)

The search for power was to be found in mystery. The figure of Lady Wisdom from Proverbs could now be extended in a Hellenistic way beyond what politics or philosophy or mystery religions could teach. Writing as Solomon, the author praises her:

Such things as are hidden I learned and such as are plain;
  for Wisdom, the artificer of all, taught me.
For in her is a spirit
  intelligent, holy, unique,...
For Wisdom is mobile beyond all motion,
  and she penetrates and pervades all things by reason
  of her purity.
For she is an aura of the might of God
  and a pure effusion of the glory of the Almighty;
  therefore nought that is sullied enters into her.
For she is the refulgence of eternal light,
  the spotless mirror of the power of God,
  the image of his goodness.
And she, who is one, can do all things,
  and renews everything while herself perduring;...
For she is fairer than the sun
  and surpasses every constellation of the stars.
Compared to light, she takes precedence;
  for that, indeed, night supplants,
  but wickedness prevails not over Wisdom.

> *Indeed, she reaches from end to end mightily*
> *and governs all things well.*
> (Wis 7:21–22, 24–27, 29—8:1)

Wisdom has soared once again while yet remaining earthbound in Solomon, the receiver of the gift. The search for true wisdom was a lover's affair, which must be pursued passionately, with diligence and fervor. Wisdom was everywhere but one needed the faith to find her. The patterns of the language are Hellenistic, but the thought is straight from the old Jewish proverbial approach. This wisdom will emerge again in the Gospel of Luke when Jesus condemns this evil generation that is seeking a sign.

> *At the judgment the queen of the south will rise with the men of this generation and she will condemn them, because she came from the ends of the earth to hear the wisdom of Solomon, and there is something greater than Solomon here.* (Luke 11:31)

The something greater is, of course, Jesus. Then Jesus speaking as wisdom denounces the scholars of the law:

> *"Therefore, the wisdom of God said, 'I will send to them prophets and apostles; some of them they will kill and persecute.'"* (Luke 11:49)

The Alexandrian Jew could walk out of his shabby ghetto into the resplendent cultured city with head held high. The pretensions of sophistication were laughable. True wisdom was honest coin, a gift.

4. A New Direction for Wisdom

Wisdom and Sirach were never accepted as authentic sacred writings by the Palestinian Jews in the homeland. Wisdom was written not in Hebrew, but in Greek, and in a foreign land. Even Sirach, although originally in Hebrew, for all its law-centeredness, was written so late that it was clearly composed after the days of Ezra, and so was not an acceptable sacred book, a book that "soiled the hands," that is, it was so sacred that it left its mark on the hands that touched it and required a ritual purification after reading it. Nevertheless, the Jews who lived outside the homeland continued to read them as part of the sacred collection, and they were accepted wholeheartedly by Christians, mostly Gentiles, who inherited them as Scripture.

We, therefore, encounter Wisdom reinterpreted realistically again in the New Testament. Paul speaks frequently of the wisdom that is the Spirit abiding within us.

> *To one is given through the Spirit the expression of wisdom; to another the expression of knowledge according to the same Spirit.* (1 Cor 12:8)

Another step was taken toward the creative Word of God in the Gospel of John. The prologue begins:

> *In the beginning was the Word,*
> *and the Word was with God,*
> *and the Word was God.*
> *...All things came to be through him,*
> *and without him nothing came to be.* (John 1:1, 3)

At the end the realistic identification is made:

> ...*because while the law was given through Moses,*
> *grace and truth came through Jesus Christ.*
>
> (John 1:17)

9

The New Testament Revelation of the Word of God

1. The Way of Wisdom in the New Testament

No wisdom books as such exist in the New Testament. However, the way of wisdom is found in many New Testament books but is often unnoticed. Rudolf Bultmann, the most notable proponent of historical criticism, began his crucial study on the subject with the proverbs in the Synoptic Gospels.[1] Proverbs were easily identified in the Gospels by their pithy form. Then Bultmann traced how these originally short sayings developed into more complicated literary forms as the Gospel writers created new situations for them and gave them new interpretations to meet current needs in the community.[2] This historical and then later sociological study done by Butltmann and other scholars revealed much of permanent value. However, their work centered on data, rather than on *function,* which is what this book seeks to demonstrate. We can look at some sampling of the ways in which wisdom thinking functioned in New Testament texts.

2. Paul's Wisdom and Worldly Wisdom

Paul is the earliest writer in the New Testament. His language is spiced with words from the wisdom vocabulary. Words such as *wisdom, wise, knowledge, know* and such occur more than two hundred times in the traditional Pauline corpus. More importantly wisdom thinking is Paul's usual way of expressing his insights.[3] Paul moves from what his readers have experienced to the insights behind the master story. He takes it for granted that his readers have heard the Jesus story and so refers to it only in the triadic phrase, "he died, was buried and was raised."[4] They knew the rest of the Good News. They had also experienced a personal conversion. In the usual wisdom way Paul moves from those slices of earthy experience to his insights of what is behind the Jesus story. His favorite way of expressing himself is by antitheses, indeed paradoxes. The coming of Jesus, the Savior, has completely reoriented the function of wisdom. It is first the gate into knowing the new people of God. Secondly, Jesus, and he alone, is the end of wisdom.

> *For Christ is the end of the law for the justification of everyone who has faith.* (Rom 10:4)

The First Epistle to the Corinthians makes capital of this approach to the way Jesus affects our lives. Some worldly and sophisticated Corinthians wanted to preach the Gospel in their own highflown philosophical language. Paul would have none of it:

> *The message of the cross is foolishness to those who are perishing, but to us who are being saved it is the power of God. For it is written:*
> *"I will destroy the wisdom of the wise,*
> *and the learning of the learned I will set aside."*

*Where is the wise one? Where is the scribe? Where is
the debater of this age? Has not God made the wisdom of the world foolish? For since in the wisdom of
God the world did not come to know God through
wisdom, it was the will of God through the foolishness of the proclamation to save those who have
faith. For Jews demand signs and Greeks look for
wisdom, but we proclaim Christ crucified, a stum-
bling block to Jews and foolishness to Gentiles, but
to those who are called, Jews and Greeks alike,
Christ the power of God and the wisdom of God. For
the foolishness of God is wiser than human wisdom,
and the weakness of God is stronger than human
strength. Consider your own calling, brothers. Not
many of you were wise by human standards, not
many were powerful, not many were of noble birth.
Rather, God chose the foolish of the world to shame
the wise, and God chose the weak of the world to
shame the strong, and God chose the lowly and
despised of the world, those who count for nothing,
to reduce to nothing those who are something, so
that no human being might boast before God. It is
due to him that you are in Christ Jesus, who became
for us wisdom from God, as well as righteousness,
sanctification, and redemption, so that, as it is written, "Whoever boasts, should boast in the Lord."*

(1 Cor 1:18–31)

3. Paul's Wisdom Concerning the Resurrection

In 1 Corinthians 15 Paul makes this wisdom of God
function in a very practical way. Some Christians were
saying that there is no resurrection of the dead. We do
not know how they reached this curious conclusion, but
we do know that it was proposed by Corinthians. Paul
had denounced some of them in the first chapter for their

puffed-up pretensions to a superior wisdom. Here Paul begins his counterattack with the names of the numerous witnesses who have seen the resurrected Jesus, including, finally, himself. That experience is certain.

In the long explanation that follows in 1 Corinthians 15:12–58 Paul uses many "wisdom words" from the old vocabulary. But then he branches into some others that we cannot trace to the Old Testament. He speaks of a "spiritual body" (15:44), of being "transformed" from seed to full-grown grain (15:51), of the corruptible being clothed with incorruptibility (15:53–54). These strange words can be found in early Jewish mysticism.[5]

A good example is the mystical tradition of describing the afterlife as a journey through stages toward perfection. Versions that flourished in rabbinic Judaism were derived from the wisdom tradition and the prophetic visions, especially of Ezekiel and Daniel. In them, the self must divest itself of earthly clothes and put on throne robes as one approaches the glory of God. This "glory" is the traditional Jewish kabod, the visible sign of the presence of God in his wondrous appearances and in the Temple. *Glory* is a favorite word with Paul.[6] For example, in 2 Corinthians 4:4 he identifies Jesus with the glory:

> *...the god of this age has blinded the minds of the unbelievers, so that they may not see the light of the gospel of the glory of Christ, who is the image of God.*

Again in 1 Corinthians 15:48–49 Paul changes the metaphor to apply to us who shall bear the image of Jesus:

> *As was the earthly one [ed. note: Adam] so also are the earthly, and as is the heavenly one, so also are*

the heavenly. Just as we have borne the image of the earthly one, we shall also bear the image of the heavenly one.

And then he goes on to explain further:

And when this which is corruptible clothes itself with incorruptibility and this which is mortal clothes itself with immortality, then the word that is written shall come about:
"Death is swallowed up in victory.
Where, O death, is your victory?
Where, O death, is your sting?" (1 Cor 15:54–55)

Was Paul skirting around the language of divinity by using the cognate language of mysticism? We cannot interpret such a passage by historical data or vocabulary study alone. We know the story of Adam and that of Jesus, but by what logical bond do we connect them with death and transformation? We know that this is metaphor, but metaphor is never a simple "this equals that." The real connection is an antithesis found in the master story of Paul's readers. Jesus, the Son of God, amazingly, suffered death and then was raised again to that eternal life of which he spoke so often. That leads us to have some appreciation of the mystery of Jesus' triumph over death and of our being clothed with immortality. As Paul had written to the Thessalonians:

For the Lord himself, with a word of command, with the voice of an archangel and with the trumpet of God, will come down from heaven, and the dead in Christ will rise first. Then we who are alive, who are left, will be caught up together with them in the clouds to meet the Lord in the air. Thus we shall always be with the Lord. (1 Thess 4:16–17)

The wisdom of God is a leap in the dark toward divinity in us. We must put off our fleshly clothes for the throne robes of the spiritual body.

3. The "Man of the Earth" in Colossians

The Epistle to the Colossians also reflects Paul's daring leap of understanding into explaining the divine and human Christ.[7] Once again in this letter we ascend to a Jesus who bestrides the earth but reaches into the heavens as the cosmic Man. The language of the epistle is heavily dependent on wisdom words.[8] Some images from the Old Testament or Paul's previous writings can be adduced, but we do not fully know the problem he was addressing. For sure, the unity of Jewish and Gentile Christians in the churches is a central point. But there are also various instigators, whether from the old Jewish Law sector or from pagan speculations about the forces that controlled the universe, people who worry about the "elemental powers of the world" (Col 2:8), the despoiling of the "powers and principalities" (Col 2:15),[9] and the "fullness" (Col 1:19;[10] 2:9), although in this last case we cannot specify the fullness that Paul must have in mind. Obviously this has aspects of apocalyptic thought, but the emphasis is not really on "the end time" but on the present reality of new life in Christ.

The christological poem near the beginning is crucial but difficult. Two parts, each different in its picture of Jesus, are given. First he is himself the "icon," the image of the Father as the "firstborn of all creation" (Col 1:15). Then he is the "head of the body" and the "firstborn from the dead" within the church (1:16–20).[11] The "image of God" is derived from the first humans in the creation story of Genesis 1. Paul now reinterprets Jesus as the creator, the firstborn of all creation:

> *For in him were created all things in heaven and on*
> *earth,*
> *the visible and the invisible*
> *whether thrones or dominions or principalities or*
> *powers;*
> *all things were created through him and for him.*
> (Col 1:16)

The second use of "image" pictures Jesus as the firstborn of the dead.

> *He is the head of the body, the church.*
> *He is the beginning, the firstborn from the dead,*
> *that in all things he himself might be preeminent.*
> (Col 1:18)

After this Paul develops his usual insight of the cosmic reconciliation (Col 1:19—2:3). His readers had their own shared experience of conversion (Col 1:24—2:3) so that all are

> *enriched with full assurance by their knowledge of*
> *the mystery of God—namely Christ—in whom every*
> *treasure of wisdom and knowledge is hidden.*
> (Col 2:3)

The thought wends its way up from the realistic picture of the buried Jesus who has been reborn and from the readers' cognate experience of conversion to the cosmic figure who supplies all our needs. The rhetoric encourages the reader to make the same leap into the mystery (1:27).[12] The earthly Jesus who was the subject of the master story of Paul has now become the cosmic

Man bestriding the whole universe, giving it existence and meaning. The little girl at the creation in Proverbs 8:27–31 had functioned in a similar way.

4. The Bread from Heaven

The sixth chapter of the Gospel of John summarizes in many ways what the Gospel is all about. Viewing the sequence as acts of a drama helps to clarify its meaning. Act 1 is the misunderstood sign of the multiplying of the loaves (John 6:1–15). Act 2 is the mysterious walking on the sea, when Jesus simply identifies himself as the I AM (John 6:16–21). Act 3 reinterprets the ancient story of the bread from heaven to make the teacher the bread (John 6:22–40). Act 4 is the crisis of decision among the hearers (John 6:41–71).

This holds together, not logically but with great persuasion for those who will dare to close the gaps between experience and new insights. The rhetoric of wisdom comes to its fruition here. The master story of the Old Testament is clearly the background of what Jesus does and says, especially the story of the feeding of the Israelites in the desert. The crowd had learned about that in the synagogue and from their elders. They were now confronted with the present experience of the multiplication of the loaves. It is not the similarities but the differences that are crucial throughout, just as Sirach had remarked: "See now all the works of the Most High: they come in pairs, the one the opposite of the other" (Sir 33:15).

The story begins with the wondrous feeding of the multitude. Unlike the other Gospels, no mention is made of Jesus' compassion for the crowd. Instead Jesus is testing the faith of Philip and the other disciples (John 6:6).

The wondrous deed is done and the crowd misunderstands the meaning of this sign. They piously say that Jesus is a prophet, but the narrator tells us that Jesus knew that they wanted him as a king. Prophets demand; kings provide a living.

In Act 2 Jesus walks on the water but, unlike the other Gospel stories, he does nothing—no stilling of a tempest, no drawing Peter out of the water. Here the disciples are rowing against the wind when they see Jesus walking on the sea. His only action is to identify himself as "It is I." Or is there more to it than that? The Greek text puts it more concisely, "I am," and that phrase, both in the Greek Old Testament and at key points in this Gospel, means God. When Moses, who had not previously been recognized as a leader among the Israelites, was sent by God to bring them out of Egypt, Moses asked the practical question:

> *"...when I go to the Israelites and say to them, The God of your fathers has sent me to you, if they ask me, 'What is his name?' what am I to tell them?" God replied, "I am who am." Then he added, "This is what you shall tell the Israelites: I AM sent me to you." (Exod 3:13–14)*

Now Jesus, who has not yet been recognized by the crowd for who he really is, reveals himself to his disciples on the sea as the I AM. With Jesus God is no longer unseen.

Act 3 continues the misunderstanding of the wonder of the multiplication of the bread. On the next day the crowd was simply interested in how he had gotten across the sea so quickly and whether they had missed another wonder.

> *Jesus answered them and said, "Amen, amen, I say to you, you are looking for me not because you saw*

signs but because you ate the loaves and were filled.
Do not work for food that perishes but for the food
that endures for eternal life, which the Son of Man
will give you. For on him the Father, God, has set
his seal." (John 6:26–27)

Seeking to justify themselves they ask for a sign. After
all, they said, Moses had given them bread from heaven
as a sign that they could believe.

What Jesus answers is cast in the form of a rabbinic
homily that depends on exact understanding of the text
plus a creative connection of meanings. First, he corrects
their misquotation that Moses had given them bread
from heaven; it was God who did so. The Israelites
should have known that the bread called manna was
simply a symbol of the teaching that they were to receive
in the desert, namely, the giving of the Law on Mount
Sinai. Their ancestors had never understood that and
neither do they. They could not or would not connect the
manna with the teaching. Jesus forced them to make a
bolder jump by far. Not only is his teaching a new bread
from heaven, but he himself is the bread that came down
from heaven (John 6:38).

They object. They know his father and mother but
they do not understand anything about his coming down
from heaven. Something more than logic is needed to
accept what he says:

Jesus answered and said to them, "Stop murmuring
among yourselves. No one can come to me unless the
Father who sent me draw him, and I will raise him
on the last day. It is written in the prophets: 'They
shall all be taught by God.' Everyone who listens to
my Father and learns from him comes to me."
(John 6:43–45)

Wisdom has always demanded the human act of imagination to close the gap between experience and insight. It was so with the picture of the girl craftsman who was with God at the creation. Yet something more than imagination and rhetoric is needed:

> *No one can come to me unless the Father who sent me draw him, and I will raise him on the last day.*
> (John 6:44)

Theologians call this drawing by the Father grace. It is a gift that is difficult to refuse, especially when one realizes the alternatives that Jesus has held out: either eternal life or grubbing for a living. It is also difficult to accept. Only faith can lead the reader to do so. In a breathtaking leap Jesus reveals not just that he is a teacher but that his earthy flesh and blood is the food that they must eat. The pursuit of wisdom has come full circle. Wisdom began on the streets of life and had tried to reach up to the heavens. Now Wisdom has come down from heaven and the flesh and blood of the One who came down from heaven must be crunched between the teeth to give eternal life.[13]

The final act can only spell out the action that rhetoric demands. "Does this shock you? What if you were to see the Son of Man ascending to where he was before?" (John 6:61–62). "Do you also want to leave?" (John 6:67). And the only answer can be one of faith, not of logic:

> *Simon Peter answered him, "Master, to whom shall we go? You have the words of eternal life."*
> (John 6:68)

The meaning of the walking on the sea had finally gotten through.

"My child, when you are ill..."
Sirach 38:9

10

In Conclusion:
The Rhetoric of Wisdom

1. The Role of Rhetoric for Persuasion

This book has been an experiment in methodology.
The commerce of daily life depends on rhetoric. Luis
Alonso Schökel called this the most important element
in "common language." We use it daily in everything
from the bringing up of children to the bringing down of
enemies. An appropriate story, a relevant image, a witty
remark that dissolves anger, the situating of a problem
within a different ambit, the appeals to self-interest—
these have always been weightier coin than logic.

Socrates despised rhetoricians as the perverters of
truth. Socrates unfortunately lost the argument. The
curious thing about rhetoric is that it alone bridges the
gaps within the paradoxes that we experience so often in
life. The attempts to prove logically that no contradic-
tions exist in a mystery are never very convincing.
Indeed, the surprise ending that does not even pretend
to explain all but seems appropriate to the mystery, or
the use of a symbol that pictures aptly some paradox but
does not prove anything satisfies us as realistic in our
experience. Thus, for example, St. Patrick explained the

Trinity to the Irish king by holding up a shamrock. The king and his followers became believers in the Father, the Son and the Holy Spirit. While the legend has no historical basis, it has served well as a symbol of identity for the Irish.

2. The Power of Metaphor

Metaphor, like proverb, cannot be precisely defined. We may as well accept the popular usage that metaphor means an image in place of an abstraction. As Leo Perdue has pointed out, metaphor has immense power to influence actions and form character.[1] Sociological studies about Catholics show that the power of the image of the Blessed Virgin Mary has not diminished among Catholics since Vatican II.[2] Andrew Greeley in a study in 1985 found those liberal Catholics who do not agree with official church teachings, especially on sexual matters, are drifting back to church attendance despite their own opposition.[3] He had no firm explanation for this but surmised that the liturgy of the Eucharist as the symbol of their deepest beliefs overrode their lesser reasons for opposition. That impressively silent moment at the consecration in the Mass is uniquely powerful for Catholic congregations. At that moment we proclaim the mystery of faith.

The image compels action. The wisdom writers denounced social evils although, unlike the prophets, they were not activists. They observed oppression of the poor, bribery and greed in government, pride among the elite; then they revealed how much all this violated the sacred wholeness of creation. By preserving the wisdom writings, the people of Israel acknowledged that they expressed the acceptable lifestyle and worldview.[4] In the Gospel of John the version of the cleansing of the Temple was not simply a social protest (John 2:13–22): "Destroy this temple and in three days I will raise it" is a pithy statement, like a proverb, that challenged the disciples to a deeper understanding. Thus the author of the Gospel, observing from his later experience, notes it was not until after Jesus was raised from the dead that the disciples finally realized he had been speaking of the temple of his body and began to believe. So did many others.

3. Its Levels of Metacommunication

Leo Perdue stressed very well that imagination is the key to creating relevant images. Watzlawick did the same in his clinical experience with sick patients who created irrelevant images based on a skewed worldview. The medieval Scholastic theologians described the perfection of God by the method of subtracting our concrete human limitations from the definition of the perfect. To define the persons of the Trinity, they reverted back to images in speaking of God as Father, Son and Holy Spirit. For our perfect life in heaven they used another image, the beatific vision. In essence, abstractions are the metacommunications of concrete images.

Shakespeare in *Midsummer Night's Dream* has Theseus the king, say:

> *"The poet's eye, in a fine frenzy rolling,*
> *Doth glance from heaven to earth, from earth to heaven.*
> *And, as imagination bodies forth*
> *The forms of things unknown, the poet's pen*
> *Turns them to shapes, and gives to airy nothing*
> *A local habitation and a name."*

His wife Hippolyta adds:

> *"But all the story of the night told over,*
> *And all their minds transfigur'd so together,*
> *More witnesseth than fancy's images*
> *And grows to something of great constancy;*
> *But, howsoever, strange and admirable."*[5]

The mind which seeks the invisible God must do so in images. The abstract is a secondary activity of our minds; the concrete is what we see and feel first.

So in Proverbs 4—9 the father begins with his own earthy experience of women, good and bad. At the end, however, he has ascended to the vision of the little girl of creation in Proverbs 8:22–36. The father does not expect his son to profit by rote sayings, but he challenges him to follow in his footsteps to discover Lady Wisdom. Without the local habitation and a name, the poem does not have power. That leap from experience to imagery has implications beyond what both the concrete image and the abstractions say.

4. The Unique Foundational Form of Proverb

The papal encyclical *Divino Afflante Spiritu* (1943) encouraged us to go back to the ancient forms in which people contemporary to the writings of the Bible expressed themselves.[6] Much of our current popular interpretation of Scripture has been fashioned from the historical critical method. It gave us an impression of reality that we could picture. Unfortunately we have discovered lately that historical criticism has become so sophisticated that scholars speak mostly to other scholars but no longer to the worshipers in the pew. Now we are beginning to bring back the tools of rhetoric. And rhetoric itself needs a vigilant watchdog to prevent it from losing its grip on reality lest the condemnation of Socrates be proven true.

The wisdom writings arose from shrewd observations of how people and nature acted and reacted. They managed to catch the tension that existed in all things— "God made all in twos, the one against the other" (Sir 33:15). The opposites could hold together only by a sense of the incongruous, the paradoxical. That made good sense as one perceived the survival of all that was good despite corruption, even the corruption of the best. Behind it all was a vision of a creating God who made all things and rejoiced in their goodness.

Proverbs are the unique foundational form of all this wisdom. People could take proverbs with a grain of salt or with a quaffing of mystery as personal experience suggested. Eventually, however, the accepted versions of a civilization's proverbs added up to a canon of wise living for the people. That wisdom allowed one to survive and then to take the great leap into the mysterious stream of life that was constantly rushing through our daily existence. To have missed wisdom was the great tragedy.

> *For the LORD watches over the way of the just, but*
> *the way of the wicked leads to ruin.* (Ps 1:6)

So the people's songbook ends its introductory keynote hymn. Awe and respect for God—or as the traditional phrase put it, "the fear of God"—is the beginning of it all. It is the only way that leads to justice, which is the wholeness of life in God and in us.

5. The Biblical Master Story and Rhetoric

I have written often of a "worldview." It is a common expression in many literatures and sciences. However, it is an abstraction. Behind our attitudes toward life lies our personal story. Whether we reflect upon it occasionally as a story with a plot or whether we ignore it, it forms the connective between our past and the future. What essentially distinguishes one people from another is their master story. Ethnic identity, land boundaries, social conditions mean less in determining what kind of people we are, personally and communally, than the story of our origins and the reason for our unity. It is so instinctive that we often do not recognize its presence. The United States is the one superpower in the world today. So we tell ourselves without much thought about what being a superpower means, how the country got there and where it is going. Our thoughts of "manifest destiny" still enthrall us even when we don't know what the destiny is. The Bible as the story of the people of God holds us together and gives us communal life.

6. Wisdom as the Gift of the Good God

Leo Perdue subtitled his book *Creation Theology*. Most scholars agree that wisdom springs from the goodness implied in our creation theology. The prophets of the Bible also perceived this but in an even more paradoxical way. True prophets are always prophets of woe and weal, both together. We tend to remember the woe more than the weal. The wise men, on the other hand, began with the good, exuberant God of creation, and then they could double back to the consequences of sin. Such are the prologue and epilogue of Job and Qoheleth's advice to young men to remember the joys of their youth but not lose sight of judgment on their lives. Even death must end with going home and growing toward experiencing more of the perfection of ourselves in the beyond. The hard slate of reality does not prevent the colors from gleaming. The people who canonized these writings knew that proverbial wisdom invited them to enjoy the challenge that the favor of God bestowed.

> *Go, eat your bread with joy and drink your wine with a merry heart because it is now that God favors your works. At all times let your garments be white, and spare not the perfume for your head. Enjoy life with the wife whom you love, all the days of the fleeting life that is granted you under the sun.*
>
> (Eccl 9:7–9)

7. The Endless Renewal of the Life of Wisdom

Sometimes as I sit meditating in the early morning, I can see the hummingbirds coming to drink at their feeder outside my window. Then come the other birds to their feeder and the squirrel who runs along the power line. The trees are verdant with the life pulsing through them. I cannot see all the other signs of life in the sky, on the ground and under the ground, but I know that a vast torrent of life is rushing all around me. And I am part of it. The fall is coming; old age is upon me, but the spring rains will bring a renewal of all life. So I meditate on the Bible.

> *My soul is downcast within me;*
> *therefore I will remember you*
> *All your waves and breakers sweep over me.*
> *At dawn may the LORD bestow faithful love*

that I may sing praise through the night,
praise to the God of my life. (Ps 42:7–9)

In keeping with the Good Shepherd imagery applied to him, Jesus said: "I came so that they might have life and have it more abundantly" (John 10:10). So in my lifetime I can join the ancient psalmist in singing the praise of the loving Lord at dawn with a saying of Jesus about abundant life and with my present experience. Rushing brooks, the Good Shepherd, the amazing life stream everywhere that endlessly renews itself are all connected. This is the power of imagination and of faith.

I have tried to connect some major images from Old Testament wisdom into the worldview of the New Testament. Most importantly, Lady Wisdom foreshadows the creative Word of God in Jesus. Our dignity as the image of God in Genesis comes back in the image of Jesus the icon of the Father in Colossians 2:15–20 and in ourselves as we are imbedded in that mystical body. The rhetorical way of interpreting the wisdom literature is not imported into the Bible; it is often the way in which the New Testament uses the Old to reinterpret the reality of Jesus.

Epilogue

Mr. John Smith carefully adjusted his bowler hat before leaving home for work. Bowler hats had come back into fashion after the Environmental Disaster of January 1, 2000. The disaster was the only one that had escaped prediction and so came as a great surprise. The earth had suddenly lost most of its gravity. Bumping into things with one's head had become common.

As he left his house, he met Joe Kelly. Joe was floating at a height of about five feet, and he had to duck. "Morning, Joe," he said affably. Joe was a homeless person who sometimes slept in Mr. Smith's front yard under the bushes. Occasionally, he forgot to keep his feet firmly wedged in the bushes, and during the night he would rise to the occasion, so to speak. The Gravity Police would be around later to pull him back—unless he floated higher and the Sky Hook Brigade was needed.

"Sleep well?" Smith asked. "You look good this morning." Mr. Smith touched his Legion of Meriting boutonniere. The Legion of Merit had been abolished as self-aggrandizing and in its place the Legion of Meriting had been established. With most of the horizontal levels of society misplaced, no one wished to be pointed out as a man who had "made it." Instead, the more respected members were those who affirmed other people as the superior achievers. The difficulty was in getting used to this kind of classless society.

Psychiatrists had been dealt a severe blow. Everyone now wore a "self-image symbol," which affirmed the accepted self-image without need for counseling. It was not Big Brother who dictated the symbols. One could choose what one wanted to wear as long as it was the proper color. Mr. Smith's was the warm brown muffler that he had carefully arranged in a loose fashion around his neck. Joe Kelly actually wore several different colors. He had several different self-images. The white one indicated that he was a Hero. The green one indicated that he was compassionate, affirming and good natured, but rarely worked. The black one warned that he was aggressive and would steal your hubcaps if you parked at the curb. He especially liked that one.

On the other hand, funeral directors had benefited. They no longer had to engage brutal men to dig graves. That had been banned since the soil tended to disperse in the air. It was much simpler just to write a scenario for the final ceremony, eulogize the departed, release the hold-downs and let the deceased float into the heavens in dignified solemnity. This ascending into heaven was the occasion of many jokes, but one could not argue with the economic advantages.

People had already coined a saying that was in danger of becoming a proverb.

> *"Who will ascend into heaven;*
> *who will hold me down to earth?"*

It met the present needs and seemed to have some sort of mystic meaning to it, though most could not tell what that meaning was. However, it did promote a spiritual revival among a sect who spoke much of angels and insisted that Satan had fallen by reason of gravity.

Oddly, people seemed to be in a better humor now that the primary law of gravity had been weakened. As he walked down the sidewalk, Mr. Smith met a pretty little girl skipping along, singing and greeting all she met. Since Mr. Smith was so formally dressed, she stopped in front of him, curtsied, smiled and said: "Good morning to you, Mr. Smith. It is a beautiful day." And then she ran off again as free as the wind and yet more comfortably earthbound than the adults. And as she left, he heard her singing:

> *When he made firm the skies above,*
>   *when he fixed fast the foundations of the earth;*
> *When he set for the sea its limit,*
>   *so that the waters should not transgress his command;*
> *Then was I beside him as his craftsman,*
>   *and I was his delight day by day,*
> *Playing before him all the while,*
>   *playing on the surface of his earth;*
>   *and I found delight in the sons of men.*

And God laughed.

Notes

1. The Underpinnings of Wisdom

1. Leo G. Perdue, *Wisdom and Creation, The Theology of Wisdom Literature* (Nashville: Abingdon, 1994); Roland Murphy, *The Tree of Life: An Exploration of Biblical Wisdom Literature* (Grand Rapids, Mich.: Eerdmans, 1990); William Brown, *Character in Crisis: A Fresh Approach to the Wisdom Literature of the Old Testament* (Grand Rapids, Mich.: Eerdmans, 1996).

2. Murphy, *Tree,* 43.

3. Watzlawick has been a clinical psychologist at Palo Alto Mental Research Institute since 1960. He is the author, with his collaborators, of numerous studies. Paul Watzlawick, Janet Beavin, and Don Jackson, *Pragmatics of Human Communication: A Study of Interactional Patterns, Pathologies and Paradoxes* (New York: W. W. Norton, 1967); Paul Watzlawick, J. H. Weakland, and R. Fisch, *Change: Principles of Problem Formation and Problem Resolution* (New York: Norton, 1974). In *Pragmatics,* 53–54, Watzlawick explains: "...every communication has a content and a relationship aspect such that the latter classifies the former and is therefore a metacommunication." Many of his examples in *Pragmatics* are drawn from the miscommunications of patients, paradox being the chief cause of misunderstanding.

4. James W. Fowler, *Stages of Faith: The Psychology of Human Development and the Quest for Meaning* (New York:

Harper and Row, 1981). Fowler uses an adapted version of the Erickson/Kohlberg/Piaget analysis. See especially chapter 23, "Form and Content: Stages of Faith and Conversion."

5. John Horgan, *The End of Science: Facing the Limits of Knowledge in the Twilight of the Scientific Age* (Reading, Mass.; Helix Books, Addison-Wesley Publishing, 1996). A more focused and realistic view can be found in David G. Stork, *Hal's Legacy: 2001's Computer as Dream and Reality* (Cambridge, MIT Press, 1997). Here computer experts evaluate whether they can presently produce or hope to produce a facsimile of the humanlike computer, Hal, from the classic movie *2001.* A high level of doubt still exists. *Newsweek* magazine (Aug. 18–25, 1997) ran a lengthy survey on the same subject under the title "Great Science Mysteries."

6. "No one has ever seen God" (John 1:18).

7. The "single theory of everything" has been around for a long time. The medieval theologians wrote books called *summa theologica,* "the sum of all theology," and since theology was the queen of sciences, it also included the other sciences. Such medieval whimsy was exemplified by the scholar who wrote the *summa theologica de omnibus rebus et aliquibus aliis,* "the theological summary of all things and some others."

8. See Nancy Clasby, "Dancing Sophia: Rahner's Theology of Symbols," *Religion and Literature,* 25 (1993): 51–65, p. 59.

9. Luis Alonso Schökel, *The Inspired Word: Scripture in the Light of Languages and Literature* (New York: Herder and Herder, 1965), 151–173.

10. *Readers' Digest,* "Towards More Picteresque Speech," Aug. 1977.

11. Leo Perdue, *Wisdom,* ch. 2, "Imagination, Rhetoric, and Social Location in Wisdom Literature," particularly "Metaphors and Theological Imagination," 59–62. This chapter begins in a promising but wordy fashion on imagination but ends with a recourse to the usual literary forms of proverb and source criticism. Perdue never completely frees himself from the mechanics of literary formalism.

2. The Character Formation of a People

1. Wolfgang Mieder concludes his introduction to *The Prentice Hall Encyclopedia of World Proverbs* (Wolfgang Mieder, ed., Englewood Cliffs, N.J.: Prentice Hall, 1986) with the standard remark, "Proverbs are the true voice of all the people." The subtitle of the introduction is: "Behold the proverbs of a people."

2. Psalm 16 is a hymn pledging loyalty to Yahweh, who is constantly present to Israelites alone. Mitchell Dahood in *Psalms I, 1–50 (AB,* 16 [1965]), suggests that the author was a converted pagan who gladly cast his lot among the Israelites. Norman Gottwald in *The Tribes of Yahweh* (Maryknoll, N.Y.: Orbis, 1979) has pictured the conquest of Palestine as a process of incorporating large numbers of pagan settlers into the Hebrew community. This has become common opinion.

3. Matthew 1:5–6 cites Rahab the Canaanite prostitute, Ruth the Moabite, and Bathsheba, who was probably a Canaanite, as mothers within the genealogy of Jesus.

4. Proverbs 22:17–24 mentions the wisdom of Amenem-ope, an Egyptian official's advice to his son presumably in a school for court employees. Proverbs 30:1–6 quotes "the words of Agur, the son of Jakeh the Massaite," which is not a Hebrew name.

5. *By the rivers of Babylon*
   we sat mourning and weeping
   when we remembered Zion.
   On the poplars of that land
   we hung up our harps.
   There our captors asked us
   for the words of a song;
   Our tormentors, for a joyful song:
   "Sing for us a song of Zion!"
   But how could we sing a song of the LORD
   in a foreign land?
   If I forget you, Jerusalem,
   may my right hand wither. (Ps 137:1–5)

6. Most of them are found in Proverbs 1–7 (1:8, 10, 15; 2:1; 3:1, 11, 21; 4:10, 20; 5:1, 20; 6:1,3, 20; 7:1 and then again in 23:15, 19, 26; 24:13, 21; 27:11; 31:2. The father is not the only educator. "Hear, my son, your father's instruction, and reject not your mother's teaching" (1:8); "Observe, my son, your father's bidding, and reject not your mother's teaching" (6:20); "What, my son, my first-born! what, O son of my womb; what, O son of my vows!" (31:2).

7. Oddly, no reference to military education occurs, although we know that tactics and discipline were understood once a standing army was created during Saul's time, about 1100 B.C.

8. The Book of Proverbs opens with, "The Proverbs of Solomon, the son of David, king of Israel" (1:1); the opening verse of Chapter 10 reads: "The Proverbs of Solomon: A wise son makes his father glad, but a foolish son is a grief to his mother"; in 25:1 we read, "These also are proverbs of Solomon. The men of Hezekiah, king of Judah, transmitted them." The tradition continues in the later Book of Ecclesiastes and the Wisdom of Solomon.

9. Paul's use of "the law" is a notable conundrum for those who would interpret it legalistically. "What then can we say? That the law is sin? Of course not! Yet I did not know sin except through the law, and I did not know what it is to covet except that the law said, 'You shall not covet.' But sin, finding an opportunity in the commandment, produced in me every kind of covetousness. Apart from the law sin is dead. I once lived outside the law, but when the commandment came, sin became alive; then I died, and the commandment that was for life turned out to be death for me. For sin, seizing an opportunity in the commandment, deceived me and through it put me to death. So then the law is holy, and the commandment is holy and righteous and good" (Rom 7:7–12). See also Romans 2:14–15; 3:31; 7:14, 16, 22–23, 25; 1 Corinthians 9:20–21; 15:56; Galatians 3:11, 19, 21, 24; 5:18; Ephesians 2:15; 1 Timothy 1:8.

10. The consciousness of the master story of Israel often stands behind the specific injunctions. So, in the Holiness

Code, we read: "When an alien resides with you in your land, do not molest him. You shall treat the alien who resides with you no differently than the natives born among you; have the same love for him as for yourself; for you too were once aliens in the land of Egypt. I, the LORD, am your God" (Lev 19:33-34).

11. Proverbs 16:2 is repeated in 21:2: "All the ways of a man may be right in his own eyes, but it is the LORD who proves hearts." A similar thought occurs in 3:6: "In all your ways be mindful of him, and he will make straight your paths"; and in 5:21: "For each man's ways are plain to the LORD'S sight; all their paths he surveys."

12. So in the Catholic Church the hierarchy styles itself ideally as *sedes sapientiae,* "the seat of wisdom," the teacher, but not the policeman.

13. Joseph Campbell, *The Hero with a Thousand Faces* (Princeton, N.J.: Princeton University Press, 1949) is Campbell's best book. See also *The Inner Reaches of Outer Space* (New York: Harper and Row, 1988), which adopts Carl Jung's "archetypes of the unconscious" and Mircea Eliade's similar "elementary ideas" to explain the monomyth. The PBS video with Bill Moyers and Joseph Campbell was published as *The Power of Myth* (New York: Doubleday, 1988).

3. The Proverb as Fundamental Wisdom

1. ANET 43, 47 n.16

2. Wolfgang Mieder, *American Proverbs* (New York: Peter Lang, 1989), 364

3. William McKane, *Proverbs: A New Approach,* (Philadelphia: Westminster, 1970) can only suggest that in Proverbs 20:4 the sluggard in the reading may be: "He asks at harvest and there is none," instead of NAB's "when he looks for the harvest, it is not there." Leo G. Perdue, *Wisdom and Creation* (Nashville: Abingdon, 1994) translates Proverbs 10:26 "As vinegar to the teeth, and smoke to the eyes, is the sluggard to those who send him [instead of "use him," as NAB

has] as a messenger." The differences do not change the basic meaning.

4. The constituents of Hebrew poetry have never been fully defined. It is too free and inconsistent to fit our formal models. Neither do we have a precise and agreed upon definition of poetry among ourselves.

5. *Random House Dictionary:* "Wit—n. 1: the keen perception and cleverly apt expression of those connections between ideas which awaken amusement and pleasure. [Final note]: See Humor." *Britannica Macropaedia* classifies wit under *comedy*. Sir Philip Sidney noted that the best laughter comes from delight, not mocking the handicapped, but poking fun at the ridiculous. All the descriptions mention that wit depends on making connections by the hearer.

6. Wit is generally defined as repartee which has linguistic grace, polish, charm, a certain directness and perhaps saltiness. It is the *mot juste*, the precise words that fit the situation. See *Encyclopaedia Britannica, Macropaedia.*

7. I would classify Proverbs 6:6 as neutral; 6:9; 15:19; and 20:4 as platitudes; and 10:26; 13:4; 19:24; 24:30-34; and 26:13–16 as witty.

8. Wolfgang Mieder, *American Proverbs.* (New York: Peter Lang, 1989), 364.

9. A similar saying is found in, "Answer a fool according to his folly, lest he be wise in his own conceit" (Prov 26:5), and the same thought is repeated in "The sluggard imagines himself wiser than seven men who answer with good sense" (Prov 26:16).

10. ANET, the standard reference, finds similarities to most of the proverbs I have quoted in "Akkadian Proverbs and Counsels," 425b. The connection is often remote and problematic. The proverbs of these people are often purely secular; sometimes they have the bite of irony. "Without copulation she conceived, without eating she became plump!"

11. *Lord* (*Yahweh* in Hebrew) is used eighty-five times in the Book of Proverbs; *God* is used only eight times.

4. The Playful Proverb

1. The inability to tie down Hebrew *mashal,* "proverb," to a single meaning is evident here. The Bible uses it in many meanings. The Psalmist sings of the fate of the rich. "My ear is intent upon a proverb; I will set forth my riddle to the music of the harp" (Ps 49:5). Luke 4:23 has Jesus quoting the proverb "Physician, heal thyself" but calls it a parable. Our English usage is no less ambiguous.

2. William Brown, *Character in Crisis* (22–23) has noted this arrangement at the beginning of his comments on the Book of Proverbs.

3. Roland Murphy, *Wisdom Literature* ("Forms of the Old Testament Literature," 13; Grand Rapids, Mich.: Eerdmans, 1981) has treated the form of proverb extensively. He is inclined to limit proverbs to sayings that have a precise form of stychs.

4. The TDNT, in the entry for "phobe," notes: *phobe,* "The fear of God occurs in a completely new form in the Wisdom literature of Israel, especially Proverbs. The predominant use of the noun *yirah* with an objective genitive form of Yahweh in Proverbs shows already that the concept of the fear of God has left the emotional realm here and become an object of reflection." Commentators frequently use "reverent awe" as an explanation for the original meaning in most cases.

5. See also Proverbs 4:3; 10:1; 15:20; 19:26; 20:20; 23:25; 28:24; 30:11; 30:17; 31:1. The equality of father and mother is noted in Proverbs 23:22: "He who mistreats his father, or drives away his mother..." and 29:15: "The rod of correction gives wisdom, but a boy left to his whims disgraces his mother."

6. Aristotle defined character in this fashion at the beginning and end of *Nicomachean Ethics,* book 2, chapter 5: "Now we must consider what virtue is. Since things that are found in the soul are of three kinds—passions, faculties, states of character—virtue must be one of these. ...If, then, the virtues are neither passions nor faculties, all that remains is that they should be states of character."

7. Isaiah 62:5 has a notable example: "As a young man marries a virgin, your Builder shall marry you; And as a bridegroom rejoices in his bride so shall your God rejoice in you." Jeremiah 3:1 also uses the image, and Hosea 2:1–8 states a central theme of his prophecy in this metaphor.

8. The craftsman mentioned in Proverbs 8:30 has endlessly intrigued scholars. The word in Hebrew is actually "craftswoman" and the context demands that. Murphy (*Tree,* 136) comments on this mysterious word *mwn,* which is definitely masculine. The reference is to wisdom, *hokmah,* which is the subject of the discourse starting with 8:12: "I, Wisdom, dwell with experience...." *Hokmah* is definitely feminine. We have no way of saying this in English. She is playing, and so we picture her as a little girl. Commentators often call this a personification of wisdom. Unfortunately, biblical language is not strong on personifying abstractions. We are accustomed to having an abstract idea such as justice clothed in an image. *The Theological Dictionary of the New Testament,* a standard resource for scholars, rejects personification in its article on *sophia.* May we ask in the later application of this to Jesus the Wisdom, is Jesus a personification of some function of God or an actual human and divine being whom we have experienced?

9. Particularly in the Gospel of John, Jesus is the descending and ascending One, as in his remarks to Nicodemus (John 3:13). In that dialogue a contrast has been going on between heaven/heavenly (3:12, 13, 27, 31) and earth/earthly (3:12, 31), both in the initial dialogue and in the final reprise by the narrator.

10. Murphy (*Tree,* 21–22) notes the wise and the fool, as various virtues (such as humility or generosity) and vices (such as dishonesty or pride) as frequent themes. He places special emphasis on proper speech as a virtue that was taught. In Proverbs 22:28 and 23:10 a curious bit of advice is given to respect the ancient landmarks of one's neighbors' fields.

11. See *ANET,* 421–424.

12. Much has been written of late about the role of imagination in systematic theology. See David Tracy, *The Analogical Imagination* (New York: Crossroad, 1981).

5. The Iracible Job

1. Research has failed to discover where Uz lay. An indefinite location to the east seems probable. The choice of Uz and of the non-Israelite name Job seems deliberate. Ezekiel 14:14, 20 link Job with Noah and Daniel as holy men. In the musical *The Wizard of Oz* the setting is "somewhere over the rainbow." The author indeed confessed that he deliberately chose Oz as a connection.

2. Who this Satan (Heb. "adversary") is remains mysterious. He is unspecified in the text except for this twice-repeated signature speech in 1:6–7 and 2:1–2. On this basis he appears to be a kind of inspector general. Yet he taunts Yahweh about his blameless man Job (1:9, 11). If not the evil Satan, he is at least a competitor—another pagan idea. Satan does not appear after the prologue.

3. Numerous proverbs refer to such a view, e.g., Proverbs 16:4, "The LORD has made everything for his own ends, even the wicked for the evil day." See also Proverbs 15:3,10; 11:27; 24:20.

4. Robert Alter and Frank Kermode, *The Literary Guide to the Bible* (Cambridge, Mass.: Harvard University Press, 1987), 283–304, "Job" by Moshe Greenberg. Greenberg on Job gives an excellent sample of true rhetorical criticism.

5. The Hebrew text here is uncertain and the NAB has had to change the order of some of the verses to make it come out in this more coherent way.

6. Greenberg ("Job," 296–97) uses Eliphaz as the principal protagonist. In the epilogue God speaks directly only to Eliphaz. Eliphaz always speaks kindly but logically from his principles and only then applies them to Job, whom he does not understand, whereas Job speaks with high passion from how he feels about God in his concrete situation and then reaches his conclusion. Job ridicules God for winning if it is only a payoff.

7. "Do not be amazed that I told you, 'You must be born from above. The wind blows where it wills, and you can hear the sound it makes, but you do not know where it comes from

or where it goes; so it is with everyone who is born of the Spirit'" (John 3:7–8).

8. William Brown (*Character in Crisis,* 108) offers his own translation of this crucial verse: "I hereby reject [my life] and am comforted concerning dust and ashes." The bracketed words, *my life,* are written in from context. Brown admits that this is simply his own rendering among many others.

9. By the Deuteronomist's history we mean all the books from Joshua to 2 Kings, namely, Joshua, Judges, 1 and 2 Samuel and 1 and 2 Kings. They are called the Deuteronomistic history because early historical critics viewed them as commentary on the commandments, statutes, laws, etc., which are characteristic of the Book of Deuteronomy.

10. Norman Gottwald, in *Studies in the Book of Lamentations* (London: SCM, 1964), comments that this endless dirge with no light of hope is the final refuge when history has become so brutal that there is no way out.

11. Stanley Price Frost, in "The Death of Josiah: A Conspiracy of Silence?" *JBL* 87 (1968), 169–182, concludes that the Deuteronomist had no explanation for the death of Josiah and so abbreviated it as much as possible. "It destroyed the premise on which all Hebrew historiography had been written" (182).

12. The legend concerning Frederick I Barbarossa, Holy Roman Emperor (1123–90) has various forms. A famous poem by the Romantic German poet, Frederick Rückert (1788–1866) pictures the "red-beard" as I described him. Another version has him sleeping in his castle at Kyffhauser, waiting to return some day. The influence of that on Hitler's Thousand-Year Reich seems clear. It has become a salvation myth.

13. John Horgan, in *The End of Science* (Reading, Mass.: Addison-Wesley, 1996), consists of interviews by the author, a senior writer at *Scientific American,* of some forty-four pure scientists in various fields. Many of them are Nobel Prize winners. Their gloomy conclusion is, as the title says, that science is approaching the frontiers of its ability to probe farther. *Newsweek* magazine (Aug. 18–25, 1997) contains a long article entitled "Great Science Mysteries." *Newsweek*

takes the attitude that the problems remain a challenge. Nonetheless, the mystery remains.

14. So the mission of John the Baptist is described in the Benedictus thus: "And you, child, will be called prophet of the Most High, for you will go before the Lord to prepare his ways, to give his people knowledge of salvation through forgiveness of their sins" (Luke 1:76–77). Salvation is triggered not by virtue on our part but by recognition of sinfulness and its forgiveness.

15. "The ancient Hebrew writers...seek through the process of narrative realization to reveal the enactment of God's purposes in historical events. This enactment, however, is continuously complicated by a perception of two, approximately parallel, dialectical tensions. One is a tension between the divine plan and the disorderly character of actual historical events, or to translate this opposition into specifically biblical terms, between the divine promise and its ostensible failure to be fulfilled; the other is a tension between God's will, his providential guidance and human freedom, the refractory nature of man." Robert Alter, *The Art of Biblical Narrative* (New York: HarperCollins, Basic Books, 1981), 33.

16. *Theodramatik* is the middle section of Hans Urs von Balthasar's triad of works synthesizing his theology. The proposal referred to here is accessible in M. Kehl and W. Loser, eds., *The Balthasar Reader* (New York: Crossroads, 1982).

17. We continue to produce anthologies of explanations of Job. Leo G. Perdue and W. Clark Gilpin, editors of *The Voice from the Whirlwind* (Nashville: Abingdon, 1992), provide one of the most recent and best. Dramatists such as Archibald MacLeish in *JB* (1958) present Job in modern dress. Gregory the Great and Thomas Aquinas have been cited as the originators of the two basic themes of suffering as medicinal and suffering within the context of God's providence. A litany of great thinkers of the past can be cited from diverse milieus such as Maimonides, Kierkegaard and Nietzchse. Every method of interpretation from the most literal or historical to the most rhetorical has been used. No biblical scholar has as

yet come up with an explanation of Job which has gained a consensus of acceptance.

6. Qoheleth, the Gentle Critic

1. Luis Alonso Schökel, *The Inspired Word* (New York: Herder and Herder, 1965), 151–75.

2. *Vanity* (*hebel* in Hebrew) has many meanings, all of which seem to center on emptiness or impermanence, such as breath, absurdity, mystery. However, it can also refer to the literary trope called riddle. See Roland Murphy, *The Tree of Life,* 62, endnote 14, for an update on this.

3. The text here has considerable difficulties. The word "timeless" fits the context as a translation, but it's adverb form, "eternally," doesn't fit. The word "displaced" in the last verse is consoling but does not say where and how God replaces the displaced.

4. Qoheleth's name seems to designate some professional position; it may have something to do with the *qahal,* the "assembly." The LXX translated it into Greek as "Ecclesiastes," which has something to do with "church." He probably lived some time in the third century B.C.—so we conjecture.

5. Qoheleth's refrain to eat, drink and be merry occurs in 2:24; 3:13; 5:17–19; 8:15; and 9:7–10. The opposite of this joy, which God gives without merit, contrasts with vanity, which is the product of human endeavor.

6. The word *habel,* the transitory breath, is very similar in concept to *ru'ah,* the life breath that vivifies all. Leo Perdue, in *Wisdom and Creation,* makes the connection but doesn't seem to know what to do with it.

7. Fear is associated with the Lord very frequently in the Bible—over a hundred times. Most often it is awe at the power of God to save or to bless. Isaiah 8:12–13 states in a time of war: "Call not alliance what this people calls alliance, and fear not, nor stand in awe of what they fear. But with the LORD of hosts make your alliance—for him be your fear and

your awe." Perhaps the best interpretation of this is Psalm 139:6, a wisdom psalm: "Such knowledge is beyond me, far too lofty for me to reach." It is never associated with the final judgment.

8. See Ewert Cousins, *Bonaventure and the Coincidence of Opposites* (Chicago: Franciscan Herald, 1978) on Bonaventure and Nicholas of Cusa as approaching the basic mysteries of Christianity by frankly admitting that diversity in unity is the key to them all. So also the major truths of faith are all paradoxes that can be accepted only on faith, not on reason. Reason makes them "fitting" or persuasive; but that is an act of rhetoric, not of logic.

9. Robert Gordis, *Koheleth: The Man and his World* (New York: Schocken Books, 1968), 84–86. Leo G. Perdue's *Wisdom and Creation* (see especially 193–242) is a more recent and well-esteemed book on the theology of wisdom literature. Perdue wants to emphasize imagination and rhetoric but in fact ends with a dull and dark picture of Qoheleth from a scientific historical viewpoint.

10. "One thing God has said; two things I have heard: Power belongs to God; so too, Lord, does kindness, and you render to each of us according to our deeds" (Ps 62:12).

11. This is a quote from Deuteronomy on God being close to his people as no other god is.

12. Katherine Dell, in "Ecclesiastes as Wisdom," *VT* 44 (1994): 301–329, reviews the rabbinic interpretations. The rabbis hesitated at first to accept Qoheleth because the book seemed to despise "work." The most important work for rabbis was reading Torah. In the end the Solomonic ascription prevailed to make it acceptable. Then (like Fowler) they posited stages of faith. The optimistic part was due to Solomon as a young man, the more traditional part was from his adulthood, the third part was from his days of repentance. He had been deceived by the demon Ashmodai, (apparently the same as Asmodeus, the demon of anger and lust), had been deposed as king, did penance and was finally restored (319). Dell does not think that source criticism justifies its canonization in the Bible. The book was accepted by popular acclaim long before

the Solomon/David ascription made it acceptable to the rabbis. Perdue and Murphy are concerned about sources, author, formal literary patterns, etc., but seem to have missed the lyricism and wit of Qoheleth. A modern representative of the common people, Robert Short (*A Time to Live and a Time to Die* [New York: Harper & Row, 1973]), a photographer (and author of *The Gospel According to Peanuts*), has given a very insightful picture of Qoheleth.

7. The Comic Story of Jonah

1. The promise of a destruction of enemies is common in the Bible, including the NT Book of Revelation. The context is always that the Lord destroys in order to protect. As the Canticle of Zechariah says: "...that, rescued from the hand of our enemies, without fear we might worship him in holiness and righteousness before him all our days" (Luke 1:75).

2. The problem of the true and false prophets is well known in OT history. The cultures of the ancient world, pagan as well as Jewish, included a religious and political dependence on prophets who claimed to speak for God. Sometimes a professional cultic group with a tradition of ecstatic prophesying existed. Amos had to deny that he was a prophet of this sort when he preached in Bethel (Amos 7:14). The danger of such professional prophecy becoming political propaganda for a government that closely allied itself with the gods is evident ideologically and in the data that we have. The resurgent nationalism of Israel that was reestablishing itself in postexilic times gave a natural push to this distortion of Israel's concept of true prophecy.

3. Not much has been written about the Book of Jonah recently on a scholarly basis. Jack M. Sasson, *Jonah* (*AB,* 24B) and Bruce Vawter, *Job and Jonah* (New York: Paulist Press, 1983) represent a historical critical approach. Vawter's point is that Jonah represents the end of prophecy as such. Phyllis Trible, *Rhetorical Criticism: Context, Method and the Book of Jonah* (Philadelphia: Fortress, 1994) is a new approach from

rhetorical criticism of the binary structure but without seeing this as the basis for humor. Outside of scholarly works, Jonah has become enormously popular in children's books.

8. Wisdom in Late Judaism

1. Robert Alter, *The Art of Biblical Poetry* (New York: Basic Books, 1985), 163–84.

2. Burton Mack, in *Wisdom and Hebrew Epic, Ben Sira's Hymn in Praise of the Fathers* (Chicago: University of Chicago Press, 1985), elaborately diagnosed these chapters in Sirach as a vision statement of what the postexilic Jewish community could believe itself to be in its priests and prophets.

3. Perdue calls them "idol satires" in Jeremiah 10:1–6; Isaiah 40:18–20; and 41:1–7; 44:9–20; and Psalms 115:3–8; 135:15–18. Wisdom 13:11–19 revives it in a biting way by describing the folly of the carpenter who uses leftover lumber to carve an idol, which he then falls down and worships.

9. The New Testament Revelation of the Word of God

1. Rudolf Bultmann, *The History of the Synoptic Tradition* (New York: Harper and Row, 1963), 69–108. Bultmann first separated and then arranged in order what he considered proverbs in the Synoptics based on a similarity with those in the OT. He gave no reason as to why they should be arranged in this fashion. The entries gradually get less proverblike as Bultmann goes along, until they become merely instances of picturesque speech. At this point they have lost the patina of aged popular sayings, which is essential. In addition to these forty-eight *logia,* Bultmann includes twenty-five more under the headings of arguments, exhortations, questions and longer passages. Yet it was on this basis that Bultmann began to identify the stages of development of Synoptic development of forms.

2. Thus William Thompson has described Matthew's Gospel as "Matthew's Advice to a Divided Community"; John Paul Heil can use the title, "The Gospel of Mark as a Model for Action"; and Mary Ann Tolbert calls her interpretation "Sowing the Gospel." This reflects the growth of historical criticism that has developed through the years from source criticism to form history and finally to redaction criticism. Redaction process seeks to define a theme in the book, which can then be situated sociologically as meeting a need of the originating time. Sometimes this results in an approach that seems to approximate narrative criticism. The difference is mainly in how the text is seen to operate in the historical past or rhetorically in the living text.

3. See James A. Fischer, "Pauline Literary Forms and Thought Patterns," in *CBQ* 39 (1977): 209–223. The research still seems to have validity.

4. Romans 6:10; 8:34; 1 Corinthians 15:3–5; 2 Corinthians 5:14–15; 2 Corinthians 5:14–15; 1 Thessalonians 4:14. Romans 6:10 and 14:9 use similar but not identical expressions.

5. Alan Segal, *Paul the Convert, the Apostolate and Apostasy of Saul the Pharisee* (New Haven: Yale University Press, 1950). Segal proposes that Paul is the earliest witness to Jewish mysticism. The basic idea of this mysticism was to describe the journey to the *kabod,* the glory of God. In the Hellenistic expresssion of this doctrine called the *Merkabah* (or the throne chariot) the son of man becomes the *metathron,* the one beside the throne of God who has the greatest *kabod*. Philo scandalized his fellow Jews by picturing Moses as divinized through the *logos* given on Sinai, and Paul uses that image in 2 Corinthians 3:7–18. 2 Enoch speaks of the journey toward God. A transformation must occur by a change of clothes that become immortal flesh. Segal finds that Paul's "out-of-body experience" in 2 Corinthians 12 mirrors the journey of this mystical tradition and that 1 Corinthians 15:42–51 is a systematic use of it. 2 Corinthians 5:1-5 speaks of an unclothing and clothing in a mixed metaphor, and Colossians 3:9–10 exhorts Christians to "put off the old man and put on the new self

which is being renewed, for knowledge, in the image of its creator being clothed as a new man." Segal proposes that Paul united the crucified but ascended Lord with the enthroned son of man in Daniel 7 and Psalm 110:1 to arrive at a concept of divinity of Christ. The concept was a unique development within the mystical tradition of Judaism both in its final stage of Jesus as the image of God and the bearer of the *kabod.* It was also unique in incorporating the saving death of the crucified messiah. This could then be applied to believers. See pp. 69 ff.

6. Paul uses *glory* some fifty-seven times in the Pauline corpus.

7. Pauline authenticity of Colossians is problematic even today. Much of the argument against it is based on vocabulary and style. Kenneth J. Neumann, *The Authenticity of the Pauline Epistles in the Light of Stylostatistical Analysis* (SBLDS 120 [1990]—Review in *CBQ* 54 [1992]): 795–96. This is a computerized study of Pauline style to determine the authenticity of the "deutero-Paulines." It compares five crucial stylistic features in the authentic Paulines with the same in Ephesians, Colossians and second Thessalonians, and then in turn with six control documents from noncanonical writings (except Hebrews). The conclusion: "...although each of the disputed letters is distinctly Pauline in style, and in fact comes closer to Paul than to any other of the comparison authors tested (each is approximately equally close to the Pauline norm), each is also different enough from Pauline style to leave open the possibility of non-Pauline authorship."

8. A surprisingly large use of the "wisdom vocabulary" shows up in Colossians; for example, "wisdom" in 1:9, 28; 2:3; 3:16; 4:15; "knowledge" in 1:9; 2:3, 10; 3:10; "know" in 2:1; 3:24; 4:1, 6; "make known" in 1:27; 4:9; "see, discern" in 2:1,18; "intelligence" in 1:9; 2:2; "mystery" in 1:26, 27, 2:2; 4:3; "fullness" in 2:9, "fulfill" in 2:10; 4:12. This is a heavy concentration of a word group and these words are central to the thought.

9. Ephesians 2:2 has a similar mysterious force opposing Christ, which is called "following the ruler of the power of the air, the spirit that is now at work in the disobedient."

10. The texts read: "For in him all the fullness was pleased to dwell" (Col 1:19), and "For in him dwells the whole fullness of the deity bodily, and you share in this fullness in him, who is the head of every principality and power (Col 2:9–10). A similar use occurs in the other Captivity letter, Ephesians 1:23, "...which is his body, the fullness of the one who fills all things in every way," and Ephesians 3:19, "...and to know the love of Christ that surpasses knowledge, so that you may be filled with all the fullness of God."

11. N. J. Wright, "Poetry and Theology in Colossians 1:15–20," *NTSt* 36 (1940): 444–463. Wright has an interesting variation on the traditional interpretation. Basically, the poem has two balanced parts, one dealing with the Creator God (monotheism), the other with the immanent God (covenant, Jesus). So this is a statement from the OT covenant and wisdom theme into a new monotheistic interpretation in the light of the Jesus event.

12. The word *mystery* occurs in Colossians 1:26–27; 2:2; 4:3.

13. "Eats this bread" (6:51, 52, 53, 54, 56; "feeds on" is used in verse 57). The Greek text has *phage* in 51, 52, 53, but in the last and most emphatic repetition in 54 and 56, the word is *trogein*. *Phage* comes from *esthien* the normal word for "eat"; *trogein* was originally used to refer to cattle munching grain, and although later used occasionally for human eating, the deliberate change seems to indicate the narrator's emphasis on the crudeness and realism of the eating of Christ's flesh. See Raymond E. Brown, *The Gospel according to John* (AB, Garden City, N.Y.: Doubleday, 2 vols, 1966, 1970) I, 283. Culpepper (*Anatomy,* 197) recognizes that "The offensive starkness of the language of 6:51–58 causes many of the disciples to turn away, but crass cannibalistic and magical interpretations of the Lord's supper are rejected." Then Culpepper gives his narrative interpretation of the passage and justifies it: "In this case, the expansion of the core symbol explodes not the symbol but the sacrament—or at least inadequate interpretations of the sacrament—with which it is associated."

10. In Conclusion: The Rhetoric of Wisdom

1. Perdue has an elaborate explanation of metaphor but in his own writing seems more comfortable with historical criticism than with imagination. See Margaret S. O'Dell, "Contributions to Old Testament Theology in the Works of Leo G. Perdue," *RSR* 24, no. 3 (July 1998): 241–45. In three recent books of Perdue, O'Dell critiques his ambivalence between a somewhat narrow historicism and his lack of insight into the provocative nature of proverbs.

2. Andrew M. Greeley, *American Catholic Since the Council: An Unauthorized Report* (Chicago: Thomas More, 1985), 79, says: "All that can be said at the present state of our knowledge about the decline in church attendance between 1969 and 1975 is that it was sharp, it was sudden, it was related to sexuality, its effect was inhibited by loyalty and by a certain kind of religious imagery and is now over."

3. See *Commonweal,* July 17, 1988, for a report entitled "A Faith Loosely Held: The institutional allegiance of young Catholics," by William Dinges, Dean R. Hoge, Mary Johnson and Juan L. Gonzales, A follow-up by these authors occurs in a report in the *New York Times,* January 25, 1999, entitled "Younger Catholics Are Vital to Growth of Church in U.S." Greeley in *The Catholic Myth* (New York: Scribners, 1990), 244, reports the same from his earlier data.

4. Qoheleth has sometimes been accused of being passive in the face of evil. He denounces wickedness in the seat of justice (3:16), the endless toil of the greedy (4:7–8), oppression of the poor by violation of their rights by high officials (5:7–8), the pretentious Temple going by the self-righteous (8:10), the seeming injustice of the wicked prospering (8:14), the folly of a fool promoted to a lofty position (10:5–6) and the reporting of dissenters to the king (10:20). He has no advice on how to protest these evils. His is a quiet way of working hard at becoming all one can be, rejoicing in good work (3:22), enjoying honest sleep instead of the rich man's troubled nights of worry (5:11) and working at pursuing wisdom (7:23–25). Especially important are his repeated refrains to "Eat, drink

and enjoy all the fruits of his labor" (2:24; 5:17; 7:15; 8:15 and, finally, his exhortation that "anything you can turn your hand to, do with what power you have in 9:7–10). His advice to the young was "to follow the ways of your heart" (11:9). Qoheleth is not passive, but the activity he recommends is honest work at what improves life at one's own level.

5. *Midsummer's Night Dream,* act 5, scene 1, lines 10–25.

6. When Pope Pius XII issued his encyclical on the interpretation of Scripture entitled *Divino Afflante Spiritu* in 1942, Catholic scholars were still hesitant to employ historical criticism, which was the standard methodology outside the church. World War II interfered with its dissemination and its quick adoption. The encyclical encouraged Catholic scholars to go back to the way in which literary forms were actually used in the time of the origins of the biblical books. It became the magna carta of biblical studies for them. Until recently historical criticism has remained the standard methodology in Catholic commentaries, both scholarly and popular.

Subject Index

Scripture Index